The Perfect Apron

The Perfect Apron

35 fun and flirty designs for you to make

ROB MERRETT

CICO BOOKS

LONDON NEW YORK

This book is dedicated to my Mum, who lovingly nurtured my creativity, Nan, Gill – the 'Best Mum, Daughter, Sister and dust-buster EVER!' – Carmen and The Infanta.

Published in 2009 by CICO Books
an imprint of Ryland Peters & Small Ltd
20–21 Jockey's Fields, London WC1R 4BW

www.cicobooks.co.uk

10 9 8 7 6 5 4 3 2 1

Text copyright © Rob Merrett 2009
Design and photography copyright © CICO Books 2009

A CIP catalogue record for this book is available from the British Library.

ISBN-13: 978 1 906525 34 7

Printed in China

Editor: Marie Clayton
Designer: Christine Wood
Photography: Emma Mitchell and Winfried Heinze
Art direction and styling: Rob Merrett
Illustration: Trina Dalziel and Stephen Dew

Contents

Introduction

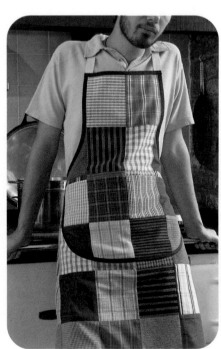

Introduction

Apparently, the apron is as old as the hills – both Adam and Eve wore one to hide from view and no doubt protect their 'naughty bits': 'And the eyes of them were opened, and they knew that they were naked; and they sewed fig leaves together, and made themselves aprons', Book of Genesis, Chapter 3, Verse 7.

More recently, the apron was traditionally viewed as an essential garment for anyone doing housework and nowadays it is enjoying a full-blown renaissance as a fun, functional and fashionable accessory for women, men and children.

For me, the apron is a sweet reminder of a gentler, more innocent time. Along with washday Monday, ironing on Tuesday, fish on Friday and Sunday school, it was a part of my childhood. Whether baking, cleaning or at mealtimes, my mum and aunts – all busy homemakers – wore a pretty pinnie, often with a little lace handkerchief stuffed in the pocket. My grandmother's choice was a straight, stricter, full-apron style reminiscent of the 30s and 40s, with a wraparound bodice that protected her dress as she fearlessly carved slices of bread dangerously close to her breast. The older generation of females in my family wore aprons not only to protect their clothing, to gently wipe away crocodile tears and because they were

practical 'holdalls' – to carry clothes pegs to the washing line in the garden, for instance – but simply because that was what you wore at home during the day in your role as a happy, soft and feminine mother, wife and carer of pets.

I hope this book recalls fond memories and you will be inspired to use it as a springboard for creating your own designs. I also hope the practical and attractive projects, plus the simple guide to basic techniques, will encourage the novice seamster and seamstress to thread a needle for the first time and start sewing.

Remember, always pin and tack before you sew and you'll get it right first time around, and if you're serious about sewing, invest in an overlocking machine, which simultaneously trims and over-edge stitches the seam allowances on a garment. The finish is neat, attractive and professional – and will save you having to make all those double hems.

Happy Sewing!

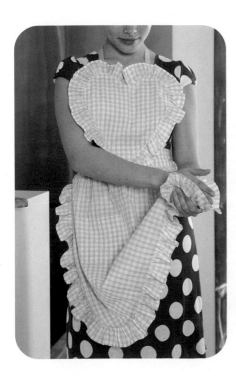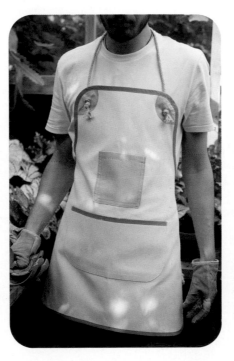

Pleat Perfection (page 12)

Plain Sailing (page 10)

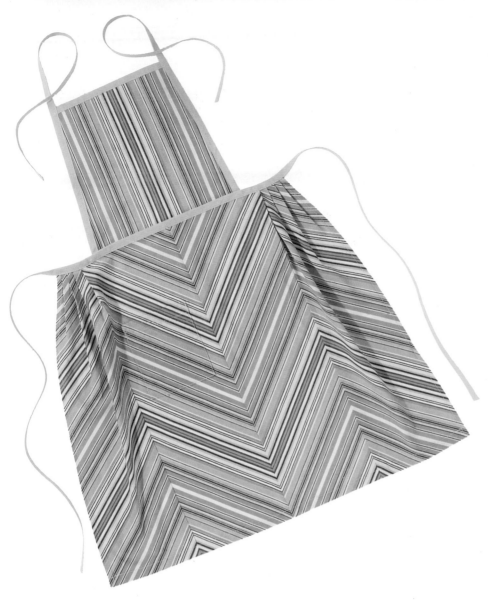

Chic Chevrons (page 16)

Back to Basics

Plain Sailing

This is a basic design for the beginner and, as the name suggests, relatively easy to make. Yet the refined ticking stripe – more beach-like when worked horizontally – and the navy blue binding create a nautical look, which is effortlessly chic. Ideal for the sporty, casual lifestyle of fashionable resorts, wear this apron with panache when dusting the yacht, washing down the deck or clam baking on the beach. 'Pass the sea-salt, dear!'

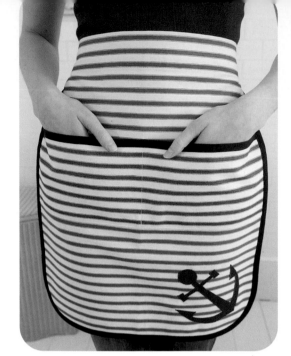

You will need:

50cm (20in) length of 144cm (57in) wide ticking stripe fabric for apron panel

50cm (20in) length of 144cm (57in) wide contrast ticking stripe fabric for pocket

190cm (76in) length of 2.5cm (1in) wide bias binding

100cm (40in) length of 2.5cm (1in) wide woven tape for waist ties

15cm (6in) BONDAWEB® (iron-on double-sided appliqué adhesive)

Tailor's chalk

Sewing machine

Needle and matching sewing threads

1.

To make the apron panel, cut out a 44 x 58.5cm (17$\frac{1}{2}$ x 23in) rectangle in ticking stripe fabric. Lay the fabric piece on your work surface with one of the sides measuring 44cm (17$\frac{1}{2}$in) nearest to you. Round off the corner at each end using tailor's chalk and the curved edge of a bowl measuring 14.5cm (5$\frac{3}{4}$in) in diameter. Remove the corners by cutting along the chalk line.

2. Make a DOUBLE HEM along the other short side of the apron panel, as described on page 114, folding over by 1.5cm (5/8in) and then by 5cm (2in) to the wrong side.

3.

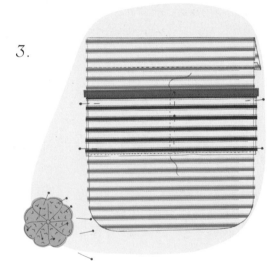

To make the pocket, cut out a strip of contrast ticking stripe fabric measuring 15.5 x 44cm (6$\frac{1}{4}$ x 17$\frac{1}{2}$in). Bind one long edge with a 45cm (18in) length of bias binding, as described in BINDING AN EDGE on page 112. Lay the pocket right side up onto the right side of the apron, 15cm (6in) below the top edge of the apron. Pin in place. Measure the centre line and run a line of pins from top to bottom. Machine stitch along the pinned line to create two pouches. Reinforce the stitching at the top edge with additional stitches.

4. To make the waist ties, cut the woven tape in half and lay one length across the wrong side of the apron, 1.5cm ($^5/_8$in) below and parallel with the top edge. Aligning the raw edges of the tie and apron, machine stitch together. Repeat for the corresponding waist tie.

5.

Cut a 145cm (58in) length of bias binding and bind three sides of the apron panel, as described in BINDING AN EDGE. Ensure the sides of the pocket and the raw edges of the waist ties are caught under the binding, and any excess at either end of the apron is neatly tucked out of view.

6. To make the anchor appliqué, trace the template on page 125 onto paper and cut out. Follow the APPLIQUÉ instructions on page 112.

Pleat Perfection

The next time you serve a sushi supper, dress for the occasion in this kimono-inspired creation, fashioned in shimmering raw silk. A blossom print cotton border and interior, plus an exaggerated bow – inspired by the knot of an obi sash – will give your guests a true taste of geisha glamour. This elegant, reversible apron style is a fusion of Eastern and Western cultures, blending a simple sporty shape with ancient Oriental influences.

You will need:

60cm (24in) length of 112cm (45in) wide silk fabric for apron front, waistband, ties and bow

75cm (30in) length of 112cm (45in) wide floral print fabric for apron border, apron back and bow

Sewing machine

Needle and matching sewing thread

Take 1.5cm ($^5/_8$in) seam allowances throughout unless otherwise stated

1. Cut out a 49 x 81cm ($19^1/_2$ x 32in) rectangle for the apron back and a 13 x 81cm ($5^1/_4$ x 32in) piece for the apron border from the floral print fabric, and a 39 x 81cm ($15^1/_2$ x 32in) rectangle for the apron front from the silk fabric.

2. With right sides together, machine stitch one long side of the apron border to one long side of the silk apron front. Press the seam allowance open.

3.

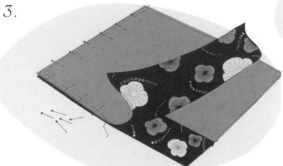

With right sides together, lay the apron back in floral print fabric onto the two-piece front panel. Aligning the raw edges, pin, tack and machine stitch along the two short sides and the one long side with the floral print border. Remember to leave the other long side open. Trim the seam allowances and turn the apron right side out. Press carefully, ensuring the apron has sharp corners and both panels are lying flat on top of each other.

4.

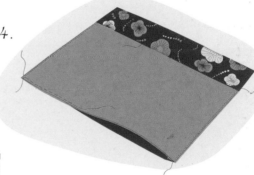

Topstitch around the apron edges at the sides and bottom. Sink a line of stitches into the seam that joins the border and the apron, and stitch the open top raw edge closed to hold all the layers in place.

5.

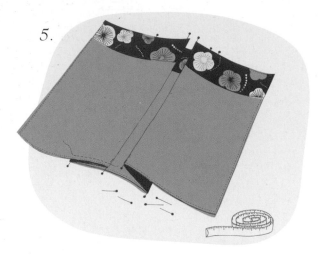

To make the central inverted pleat, measure 23cm (9^1/$_4$in) in from each edge, then a further 8cm (3^1/$_4$in) in from these two points along both the hem and the top raw edge of the apron, and mark all four points with pins at each edge. Align the corresponding pins at top and bottom by making four vertical folds. Press in the pleats with an iron, securing them at the top edge with machine stitches.

6. Cut out a 15 x 49cm (6 x 19^1/$_2$in) rectangle of silk fabric for the waistband. Cut out another two 11 x 60cm (4^1/$_2$ x 24in) strips of silk fabric for the waist ties, and follow the instructions for WAISTBAND – WITH WAIST TIES on page 119.

7.

To make the tailored bow, cut out one 7 x 100cm (2^3/$_4$ x 40in) strip from the floral print fabric and one from the silk fabric. With right sides together, stitch along both long edges, leaving the short ends open. Turn right side out and steam-press flat. Cut off a 16cm (6^1/$_2$in) piece of band and put to one side. Fold the remaining length in half and mark the point with a pin.

8. Machine stitch through all layers 24cm (9^1/$_2$in) in from the centre fold. Open out the loop you have made by stitching the band together, align the centre pin with the opened seam, and machine stitch through the join. Fold the two free ends of the band back onto themselves and place them over the centre seam, overlapping each one by 5mm (^{1}/$_4$in). Machine stitch in place.

9. Wrap the remaining piece of 16cm (6^1/$_2$in) band around the loop to form a tailored bow and secure with a few stitches at the back. Hand stitch the bow to the apron, placing it over the seam where the apron is joined to the waistband.

Chic Chevrons

Horizontal stripes evoke a jaunty, nautical mood and vertical stripes are de rigueur if you want to create a slimming effect, but by far the most fun, flirtatious and flattering way of wearing them is on the bias, or 'on the cross', as they appear to follow the body's gentle curves in the most delightful way. For a more dramatic effect, the stripes featured in this style are cut on the bias, and the panels stitched together to create a novel zigzag pattern. The simpler the stripe pattern, the easier it will be to match up when laying out your paper pattern and sewing the fabric pattern pieces together.

You will need:

100cm (40in) length of 112cm (45in) wide printed stripe cotton fabric for apron, bib and pocket

310cm (124in) length of 2.5cm (1in) wide bias binding for waistband/waist ties, bib and neck ties

Pattern paper

Sewing machine

Needle and matching sewing threads

Take 1.5cm ($^5/_8$in) seam allowances throughout unless otherwise stated

1.

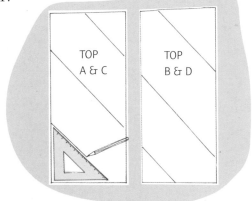

To make the apron pattern, draw two 18 x 52.5cm ($7^1/_4$ x 21in) rectangles onto paper and cut out. Write 'TOP – A & C' at the top along one of the short sides of one of the rectangles and 'TOP – B & D' in the same position on the other paper pattern piece. Draw diagonal 'stripe guide/fabric grain' lines at a 45° angle, from bottom right to top left across both pattern pieces.

2.

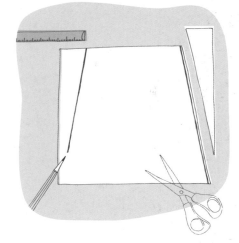

To make the tapered bib pattern, draw a 25cm (10in) square onto paper and cut out. Taking one of the sides as the top edge of the bib, measure in 2.5cm (1in) at both ends. From each of these points, draw a line down to the corresponding corners at bottom left- and right-hand corners. Cut along each line to taper the pattern piece.

3.

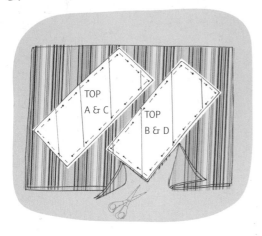

Fold your fabric in half widthways, ensuring the stripes at both ends match up exactly. Lay the two apron pattern pieces diagonally onto the fabric, lining up the 'stripe guide' lines on the paper patterns with the printed stripe of the fabric and ensuring the matching stripes under each paper pattern fall in exactly the same place. Pin and cut out through both fabric layers.

4.

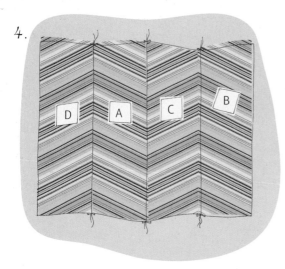

Carefully remove the paper patterns from the fabric panels to avoid separating the layers. Pin a paper note marked A to the right side of one double layered panel and a paper note marked C to its twin. Repeat for the other double-layered panel, labelling one piece B and the other D. Separate the panels and, with right sides up, lay them out in a row on your work surface in D, A, C and B sequence. Carefully pin and tack the panels together, ensuring the stripes are well matched.

5.

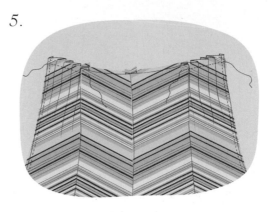

Machine stitch the panels in place. DOUBLE HEM the apron sides, as described on page 114, turning under by 6mm ($^1/_4$in) and then by 9mm ($^3/_8$in). DOUBLE HEM the bottom edge of the apron, turning under by 1.5cm ($^5/_8$in) each time. Make four 1.5cm ($^5/_8$in) deep pleats at the top of panels D and B, securing with machine stitches 5mm ($^1/_4$in) in from the raw edge. To make the apron bib, pin the paper pattern to the fabric with the stripes vertical, and cut out.

6.

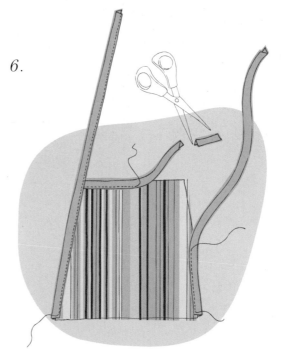

Cut a 20cm (8in) length of bias binding and bind the top edge of the bib, as described in BINDING AN EDGE on page 112, trimming the ends so they follow the line of the bib sides. For the neck ties, cut two 70cm (28in) lengths of bias binding and bind the left and right sides of the bib with one end of each. Pin and tack along the length of the bindings and close with machine stitches, overlapping the ends to finish.

7. With wrong sides together and aligning raw edges, lay the bib onto the apron. Pin, tack and machine stitch together, 5mm (³/₁₆in) in from the edge.

8.

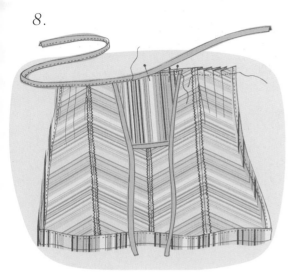

To make the 'all-in-one' waistband/waist ties, cut a 150cm (60in) length of bias binding, fold it in half and mark the centre point with a pin. Neatly insert the edges of bib and apron into the folded binding, ensuring the pin is at the centre front of the apron. Pin and tack the open edges along the length of the binding, then machine stitch along the whole length of the binding, attaching the waistband to bib and apron and closing the binding in one action. Overlap and stitch the ends of the waist ties to finish.

9. To make the patch pocket, cut out a 13 x 17cm (5¹/₄ x 6³/₄in) rectangle on the cross from the remaining stripe fabric. DOUBLE HEM one short edge, turning under by 1.5cm (⁵/₈in) and then by 2cm (⁷/₈in). Pin, tack and machine stitch in place. Fold the three remaining edges over by 1.5cm (⁵/₈in) and press. Pin and tack the pocket to the apron, matching the diagonal stripes as carefully as possible, and topstitch in place.

China Doll (page 34)

Calypso (page 30)

Hot Lips (page 22)

Rue Cambon (page 24)

La Parisienne (page 26)

Cocktail Hour (page 28)

chapter 2

Kitchen Couture

Hot Lips

Dramatic, tongue-in-cheek appliqués transform this simple apron into an artwork. Luscious, carmine-coated lips caress the front of this cover-up, giving an all-knowing wink to Salvador Dali and the witty, irreverent, Surrealist-inspired creations of couturier Elsa Schiaparelli. This is a perfect Valentine gift, so all you men out there – sign up to sewing classes now.

You will need:

75cm (30in) length of 112cm (45in) wide plain dark cotton fabric for the apron, frill, waistband and ties

3 x 10cm (4in) lengths of 110cm (44in) wide plain cotton fabric in bright tonal colours for the appliqués

225cm (90in) length of 2.5cm (1in) wide satin ribbon

25cm (4in) BONDAWEB® (iron-on double-sided appliqué adhesive)

Cotton embroidery thread

Sewing machine

Needle and matching sewing threads

Take 1.5cm (⁵⁄₈in) seam allowances throughout unless otherwise stated

Note:

A pair of sharp embroidery scissors is essential to cut neatly around the lip motifs with ease.

1.

Using apron pattern A in the pull-out section, pin the pattern to the plain dark cotton fabric and cut out the apron. Along the straight top raw edge of the apron, make a fold 10cm (4in) in from each edge, and pleat 2.5cm (1in) deep towards the centre front, so that the raw edge measurement is 38cm (15in). Pin and machine stitch the pleats in place.

2. To make the lip appliqués, trace the templates on pages 124–125 onto paper and cut out. Follow the Appliqué instructions on page 112.

3. Cut out three 6 x 77cm (2¹⁄₂ x 31in) strips of plain dark cotton fabric for the frill. Machine stitch together to make one long piece. Zigzag stitch or trim the seam allowances with pinking shears to stop the edges fraying.

4.

Bind one long edge of the fabric strip with a 225cm (90in) length of satin ribbon as described in Binding An Edge on page 112. Gather the other long edge by hand or machine as described on pages 114–115. With right sides together, aligning the raw edges, lay the frill along the apron edge. Pin, tack and machine stitch in place.

5. Cut out a 15 x 49cm (6 x 20in) rectangle of fabric for the waistband and two 9 x 48cm (3¹⁄₂ x 19in) strips for the ties. Follow the instructions for Waistband – With Waist Ties as described on page 119.

6.

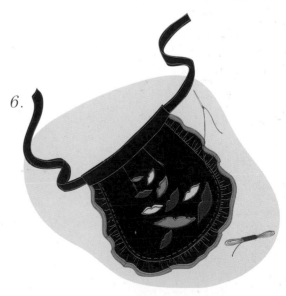

With a needle and contrast embroidery thread work a line of wide running stitch on the right side of the apron, alongside the seam that joins the apron and frill.

Rue Cambon

In homage to Coco Chanel, this icon of 50s housewifery, borrows some of her trademark touches – the contrast binding and the petite cardigan-style pockets. If you really must go the whole nine yards, add the ubiquitous gold chain to the waistband. Take your time when applying the bindings as a neat finish will make all the difference. Although smart and practical, with two handy pockets, this apron is probably not the best style to wipe your hands on.

You will need:

50cm (20in) length of 110cm (44in) wide linen fabric for apron and pockets

318cm (127in) length of 2.5cm (1in) wide woven tape in contrast colour for trim and waist ties

2 small decorative gold buttons

Sewing machine

Needle and matching sewing threads

Take 1.5cm ($^5/_8$in) seam allowances throughout unless otherwise stated

Note:

A beige apron with a red tape trim would be an alternative chic colour combination.

1.

To make the apron panel, cut out a 41.5 x 53cm (16$^1/_2$ x 21in) rectangle from the linen fabric. Lay the fabric piece on your work surface right side up and fold over 1.5cm ($^5/_8$in) to the right side along one long edge and the two short sides, and press. Cut a 128cm (51in) length of woven tape and lay it over the three folded sides of the apron to create a frame effect, making sure all edges are aligned and the corners are neatly folded and finished. Machine stitch the tape in place.

2. Using the pocket pattern 5 on page 126, pin the pattern to a double layer of linen fabric and cut out two pockets.

3.

Along the top edge of one pocket, fold over 1.5cm ($^5/_8$in) to the right side and press. Cut a 13cm (5$^1/_4$in) length of woven tape and lay it over the fold, ensuring both edges are aligned, then stitch the tape in place. Repeat for the other pocket. Fold under 1.5cm ($^5/_8$in) to the wrong side on the three remaining sides of each pocket, carefully pleating excess fabric on the rounded corners. Steam-press flat. Position the two pockets on top of the apron, pin, tack and machine stitch in place as close as possible to the pocket edges. Sew a decorative button onto the centre of the trim of each pocket.

4.

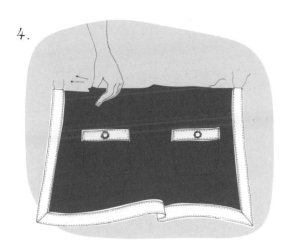

Fold the apron in half vertically to locate the centre front and mark with a pin. Measure 12cm (4³⁄₄in) out from the centre fold along the top raw edge of the apron and make a small notch in both fabric layers. Open out the apron and make a 2cm (⁷⁄₈in) deep pleat at each notch. Pin the pleat in place and topstitch it down close to the folded edge for 3.5cm (1³⁄₈in). Repeat for the other pleat.

5.

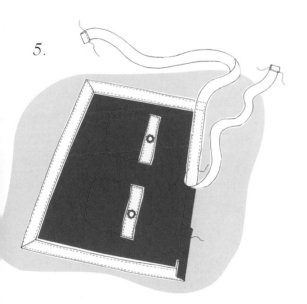

Fold over 1.5cm (⁵⁄₈in) to the right side along the top raw edge of the apron and press. Cut a 164cm (65¹⁄₂in) length of woven tape, mark the centre point, and lay it over and across the top edge of the apron, matching the centre points of the tape and apron. Pin and tack the tape to the apron and machine stitch together, stitching as close to the edges of the tape as possible. Reinforce both sides of the waistband by stitching a 'crisscross' box on each side where the apron ends. Make a DOUBLE HEM, see page 114, at the ends of the waist ties to finish.

La Parisienne

The apron worn by the waitress who served me coffee in a Viennese café many moons ago inspired this perky little style. Although the origin of the design is Austrian rather than French, its cheeky short skirt, playful bib and not-so-innocent eyelet frill bring to mind the parlour maids of bygone 'Gay Paree'! Both pretty and practical, it is an ideal featherweight cover up for light chores around the home.

You will need:

55cm (22in) length of 140cm (56in) wide printed cotton fabric for apron, bib and waist ties

368cm (147in) length of 4cm (1½in) wide cotton eyelet trim

140cm (56in) length of 1.5cm (⅝in) wide woven tape for neck ties

Pattern paper

Tailor's chalk

Sewing machine

Needle and matching sewing threads

Take 1.5cm (5/8in) seam allowances throughout unless otherwise stated

1. To make the apron panel, cut out a 31 x 59cm (12½ x 23½in) rectangle in the printed cotton fabric. Place it with a side measuring 59cm (23½in) nearest to you. Round off a corner at each end using tailor's chalk and the curved edge of a bowl 14.5cm (5¾in) in diameter, then cut along the chalk line. On the opposite edge make three, evenly spaced 1.5cm (⅝in) deep pleats at both ends, securing with machine stitches 1cm (½in) in from the raw edge.

2.

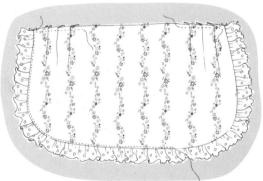

Cut a 220cm (88in) length of eyelet trim and gather to half its length by hand or machine, following the instructions for GATHERING — BY HAND on page 114 or GATHERING — BY MACHINE on page 115. With right sides together and raw edges aligned, lay the eyelet frill around the edge of the apron. Pin, tack and machine stitch in place. Zigzag stitch or trim the seam allowances with pinking shears to stop the edges fraying. Press flat on the apron side and topstitch close to the folded edge where apron meets frill.

3. To make the tapered bib pattern, draw a 26.5 x 28cm (10½ x 11¼in) rectangle onto paper and cut out. Taking one of the shorter sides as the top edge of the bib, measure in 3cm (1¼in) at both ends. From each of these points, draw a line down to their corresponding corners at bottom left and bottom right. Cut along both lines to taper the pattern piece and use an eggcup to round off the top corners.

4.

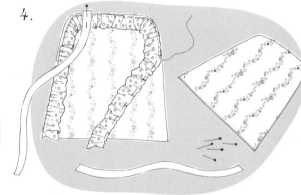

Pin the paper pattern to a double layer of the remaining fabric and cut the bib twice. Cut a 148cm (59in) length of eyelet trim and GATHER to half its length. With right sides together, and raw edges aligned, lay the eyelet frill around the top and sides of one bib piece. Pin, tack and machine stitch in place. Cut two 70cm (28in) lengths of woven tape and attach one at each side of the bib's top edge. With right sides together, lay the other bib piece on top, sandwiching the frill and neck ties. Aligning raw edges, pin, tack and stitch along the sides and top. Trim the seam allowances, snip into the rounded corners and turn right side out. Press and topstitch close to the folded edges where bib meets frill.

5.

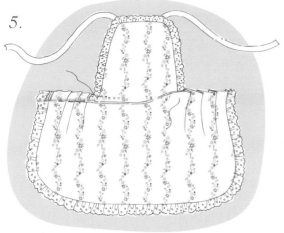

Fold the apron and bib in half lengthways, and snip a small notch into the edge of the fabric to mark the centre front points. Lay the bib onto the apron, wrong sides together, aligning the raw edges and matching up the centre front notches. Pin, tack and machine stitch together, 1.5cm (5/8in) in from the edge.

6.

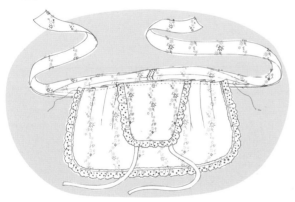

To make the two-piece, 'all-in-one' waistband/waist ties, cut out two 9 x 78cm (3 1/2 x 31 1/4in) strips of printed cotton fabric. With right sides together, join the two pieces to create a strip measuring 153cm (61 1/4in). To attach the waistband to the apron skirt and bib, follow the instructions as described in WAISTBAND – TWO-PIECE/ALL-IN-ONE on page 118.

Cocktail Hour

Be the 'Hostess with the Mostest' with this glamorous mini-pinnie. Guaranteed to turn heads, this glittering 'entrance-maker' will give your little black dress an added shot of chic. Refined, tailored bows provide the finishing 'couture' touch. For more low-key occasions, reverse your cocktail cover-up to reveal a demure sheer layer that will soften the sparkle.

You will need:

50cm (20in) length of 112cm (45in) wide brocade fabric for apron panel and waistband

60cm (24in) length of 112cm (45in) wide sheer fabric for apron panel and ties

76cm (30½in) length of 2cm (⅞in) wide satin ribbon

Sewing machine

Needle and matching sewing threads

Take 1.5cm (5/8in) seam allowances throughout unless otherwise stated

1. Cut out a 37.5 x 56cm (15 x 22½in) rectangle of brocade fabric and a 40.5 x 56cm (16 x 22½in) rectangle of sheer fabric. Make a DOUBLE HEM as described on page 114, folding over 1.5 cm (⅝in) and then another 1.5 cm (⅝in) along both short edges and one long edge of each panel.

2. Copy pocket pattern 1 on page 120 onto paper and cut out. Use the paper pattern to cut out two pockets from brocade fabric and two from sheer fabric. Using one brocade pocket piece and one sheer pocket piece, make two pockets as described in PATCH POCKETS – BAGGED OUT on page 115. Place one pocket onto the right side of the brocade panel. Pin, tack and machine stitch in place, stitching as close as possible to the edge of the pocket. Repeat for the sheer panel.

3.

Lay the brocade panel on your work surface wrong side up. Place the sheer panel right side up on top of the brocade, aligning the raw edges. Pin, tack and machine stitch along the width of the apron 5mm (¼in) in from the top raw edge. GATHER the top of the apron to 36cm (14in) by hand or machine as described on pages 114–115.

4.

Cut a 13 x 39cm (5 x 16in) rectangle of brocade fabric and make the waistband as described in WAISTBAND – BASIC on page 117, pinning the unstitched right side of the waistband to the brocade side of the apron.

5.

To make the waist ties, cut out two 13 x 63cm (5 x 25in) strips of sheer fabric. DOUBLE HEM the long edges of the strips, folding over by 5mm (¹/₄in) and then by 12mm (¹/₂in). Pin, tack and machine stitch in place, stitching as close as possible to the folded edge. Repeat on one short end of each waist tie. Concertina-fold the unhemmed end of one of the waist ties into three equal parts and pin to one side of the inner waistband. Stitch vertically in place, trim the selvedge, fold the waist tie back on itself and machine stitch again, making sure the trimmed selvedge is no longer visible. Repeat with the remaining waist tie.

6. Cut two 32cm (13in) lengths of satin ribbon and two 6cm (2¹/₂in) lengths of ribbon and make two tailored bows as described in BOWS – TAILORED on page 113. Hand stitch a bow onto each pocket.

Calypso

This knock-out apron takes its cue from warmer climes. Inspired by the sari and sarong, and exuberantly coloured and pattern-blocked, this three-piece wraparound style will transport you to a tropical paradise, where it could easily double as a chic, après-swim cover-up for beach… or lagoon. Look out for bold polka dots and madras checks, exotic jungle florals, Indonesian batiks and ethnic tribal stripes, and clash them with abandon. Keep the colours in check, however – settle for just one or two prominent hues throughout – and throw in some plains or the end result could be more Coco the Clown than Castaway Couture!

You will need:

50cm (20in) length of 112cm (45in) wide bold tropical floral print fabric

50cm (20in) length of 112cm (45in) small sprig floral print fabric

55cm (22in) length of 112cm (45in) madras check fabric

50cm (20in) length of 112cm (45in) wide polka dot fabric

50cm (20in) lengths of 112cm (45in) wide of two plain fabrics in contrasting colours

500cm (200in) length of 2.5cm (1in) wide bias binding for waist ties

112cm (45in) length of 2.5cm (1in) wide bias binding for armholes

Sewing machine

Needle and matching sewing threads

Take 1.5cm (⁵/₈in) seam allowances throughout unless otherwise stated

1.

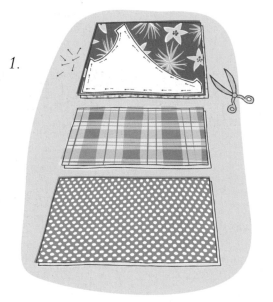

Cut out two 48 x 58cm (19 x 22³/₄in) rectangles, one in tropical floral print fabric and the other in sprig floral print fabric. Lay the rectangles wrong sides together. Using front bodice pattern C in the pull-out section, pin the front bodice pattern to the fabric and cut out.

2. For the upper left and right front panels of the apron skirt, cut out two 43 x 55cm (17 x 22in) rectangles, one in plain fabric and the other in madras check fabric. For the lower left and right front panels of the apron skirt, cut out two 45 x 55cm (18 x 22in) rectangles, one in polka dot print fabric and the other in plain fabric.

3.

Cut out a 52 x 54cm (20¹/₂ x 21¹/₂in) rectangle in madras check fabric. Taking the shorter length and with the wrong sides together, fold the fabric in half. Using back bodice pattern C in the pull-out section, pin the back bodice pattern to the folded fabric and cut out.

4. For the upper back panel of the apron skirt, cut out a 43 x 51cm (17 x 20¹/₄in) rectangle in sprig floral print fabric. For the lower back panel of the apron skirt, cut out a 45 x 51cm (18 x 20¹/₄in) rectangle in tropical floral print fabric.

5.

Taking the two front bodice pieces and the four rectangles measuring 55cm (22in) wide, assemble the left and right sides of the apron in the order of fabric patterns illustrated. Taking the back bodice piece and the two rectangles measuring 51cm (20¼in) wide, assemble the back apron in the fabric pattern order illustrated.

6. Cut out a 21 x 28cm (8¼ x 11in) rectangle for the patch pocket. At the top make a DOUBLE HEM, as described on page 114, turning under by 2.5cm (1in) each time. Turn under 1.5cm (⅝in) on the remaining three sides and pin, tack and machine stitch to the right upper front panel of the apron.

7.

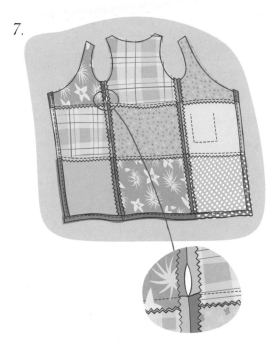

With right sides together, machine stitch the right front panel to the apron back, leaving a 3cm (1¼in) gap in the stitching (for the left waist tie to pass through), starting from the point where the upper panel seam meets the bodice. With right sides together, machine stitch the left front panel to the apron back.

8. DOUBLE HEM the vertical raw edges of the left and right front panels and the bottom edge of the apron, along its whole length, turning under by 1.5cm (⅝in) each time.

9.

Cut two 250cm (100in) lengths of bias binding and join together. Align the join with the centre back neck of the apron and neatly insert the curved edges of the left and right bodice into the folded binding, as described in BINDING AN EDGE on page 112. Pin and tack the length of the binding and, in one action, machine stitch closed. Overlap and stitch the ends of the waist ties to finish.

10.

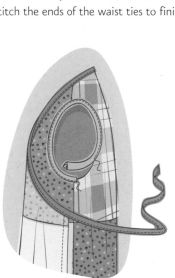

Bind each armhole of the apron with a 56cm (22¼in) length of bias binding, ensuring the ends of the bindings are neatly tucked under.

11. Using leftover bias binding, make a small belt loop (to hold in place the wraparound waist ties) and attach to the centre back at the point where the upper panel seam meets the bodice.

China Doll

The refined blues and whites of antique porcelain may be less obvious colour choices than imperial red and gold for an oriental-inspired apron, but the result is equally dramatic and evocative of the history, traditions and culture of this fascinating part of the world. Here, in fact, there is a fusion of cultures, as the origins of the cummerbund waist featured in this style are Indian. However, this attractive gathered sash adds to the drama and opulence created by the splendid pair of intertwining dragons.

You will need:

Vintage tourist shirt (Size XL) for apron

60cm (24in) length of 112cm (45in) wide plain fabric for cummerbund and ties

150cm (60in) length of 2cm (⁷⁄₈in) wide bias binding

Sewing machine

Needle and matching sewing thread

Take 1.5cm (⁵⁄₈in) seam allowances throughout unless otherwise stated

1. Unpick the back panel of the shirt and steam-press out any folds. Using apron pattern A in the pull-out section, pin to the fabric and cut out.

2.

Fold over lengthways a 150cm (60in) length of bias binding, gently steam-pressing as you fold. Bind the raw edge of the apron as described in BINDING AN EDGE on page 112.

3. Cut out a 27 x 43cm (10¹⁄₂ x 17in) rectangle for the gathered cummerbund and two 11 x 43cm (4¹⁄₂ x 17in) strips for the cummerbund backing and the back waistband in plain fabric.

4.

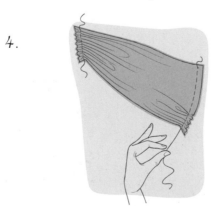

Measuring 12mm (¹⁄₂in) in from the edge, gather both short ends of the cummerbund panel to a length of 8cm (3¹⁄₄in), ensuring the gathers are 1.5cm (⁵⁄₈in) short of the panel at each end.

5.

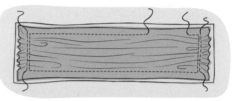

With wrong sides together, lay the cummerbund on top of the cummerbund backing. Aligning the raw edges on all sides, pin, tack and machine stitch the pieces together.

6. To make the waist ties, cut out two 15 x 70cm (6 x 28in) strips in plain fabric and follow the steps described in WAIST TIES – QUICK 'N' EASY on page 119.

7.

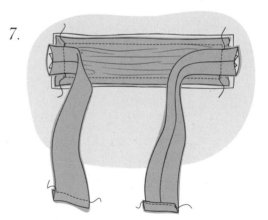

With right sides together, pin a waist tie to one side of the cummerbund and stitch vertically in place. Repeat with the remaining waist tie.

8.

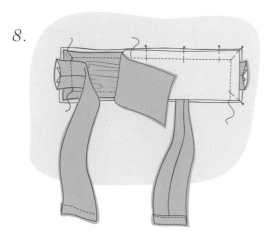

With right sides together and aligning the raw edges, lay the back waistband piece on top of the cummerbund. Pin, tack and machine stitch along both sides and the top edge, leaving the bottom edge open.

9. To attach the waistband to the apron, follow steps 3 and 5 in WAISTBAND – BASIC on page 117.

Venetian Vacation (page 44)

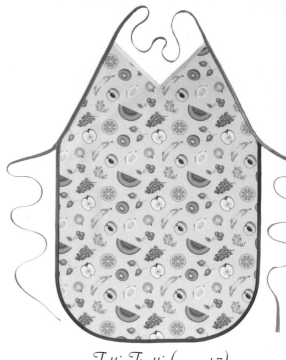

Tutti-Frutti (page 47)

Sweetie Pie (page 42)

Raspberry Ruffle (page 54)

Petal Power (page 52)

Gypsy Spirit (page 38)

Hawaiian Tropic (page 50)

chapter 3

Domestic Bliss

Gypsy Spirit

A charming full apron with a flurry of frills, which twists provocatively around the hips to the small of the back. The choice of a polka dot print for the fabric and the colour red for the frill binding, plus the heart-shaped patch pocket, evoke the passion and spontaneity of the flamenco danced by Andalusian gypsies.

You will need:

100cm (40in) length of 112cm (45in) wide polka dot fabric for the apron, frill and pocket

755cm (300in) length of 2.5cm (1in) wide red bias binding

16 x 16cm ($6^1/_2$ x $6^1/_2$in) medium-weight iron-on interfacing

Sewing machine

Needle and matching sewing threads

Take 1.5cm ($^5/_8$in) seam allowances throughout unless otherwise stated

1. Using apron pattern D in the pull-out section and pocket pattern 4 on page 120, pin both patterns to the polka dot fabric and cut out. Using the remaining fabric, cut three 6.5 x 100cm ($2^1/_2$ x 40in) strips for the frill. Machine stitch the strips together to make one long length. Zigzag stitch or trim the seam allowances with pinking shears to stop the raw edges fraying.

2. Cut a length of bias binding 294cm ($117^1/_2$in) long and use it to bind one long edge of the frill as described in BINDING AN EDGE on page 112. GATHER the other edge of the frill to 136cm (54in) by hand or machine as described on pages 114–115.

3.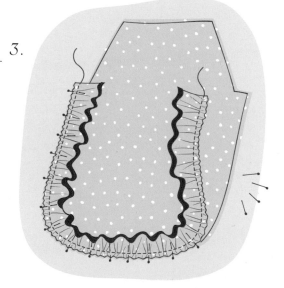

With right sides together, aligning the raw edges, lay the frill along the curved apron skirt. Pin, tack and machine stitch in place. Zigzag stitch or trim the seam allowances with pinking shears to stop the edges fraying.

4. Bind the top raw edge of the bib with a short length of bias binding. Trim the ends so they follow the diagonal line of the bib's edges.

5.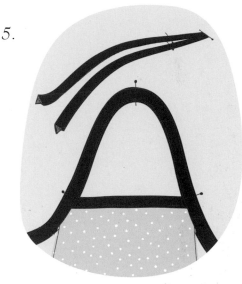

For the 'all-in-one' neck strap/waist ties, fold over a 300cm (120in) length of bias binding along its length, gently steam-pressing as you fold. Fold the binding in half and mark the centre point with a pin. Measuring 34cm ($13^1/_2$in) out from each side of the centre point, mark these positions with pins. To attach the 'all-in-one' neck strap/waist ties to the apron, align the top bound edge of the bib with the two pins at either side of the centre point pin. At these points, insert the top corners of the apron bib into the folded binding and re-pin.

6.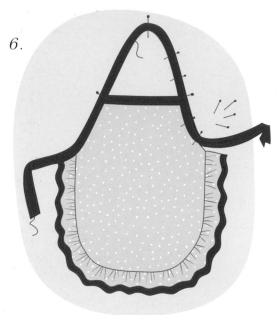

7.

Neatly insert the remaining edges of the left and right bib and frill into the folded binding. Pin and tack along the whole length of the binding and, in one action, machine stitch the apron in place and close the binding. Overlap and stitch the ends of the waist ties to finish.

Cut out a pocket in medium-weight iron-on interfacing and stick it to the wrong side of the fabric pocket. Bind the raw edges of the pocket with bias binding, carefully maintaining the curves of the heart shape.

8. To make the crisscross bows, cut two 30cm (12in) and two 5cm (2in) lengths of bias binding. Follow the steps for Bows – Crisscross on page 113. Attach one bow to the pocket and the other to the apron bib.

9. Pin and tack the pocket to the apron, ensuring that any leftover binding is neatly tucked under the pocket. Sink machine stitches through both the pocket and apron layers. Start by stitching across the binding, and then continue around the pocket, stitching over the existing topstitching of the binding. Finish by again stitching across the binding.

Sweetie Pie

This jolly full apron is the perfect cover-up for kids to wear when baking with the grown-ups. Playful patterns such as rock candy flowers and candy cane stripes enliven this style, with its dainty patch pocket for keeping a rolling pin and cookie cutters close at hand.

You will need:

45 x 50cm (16 x 20in) piece of floral print fabric for apron

20 x 25cm (8 x 10in) piece of contrast floral print fabric for pocket

15cm (6in) length of 114cm (45in) wide stripe fabric for frill

250cm (100in) length of 2.5cm (1in) wide bias binding

Sewing machine

Needle and matching sewing threads

Take 1.5cm (⁵⁄₈in) seam allowances throughout unless otherwise stated

1. Using apron pattern G in the pull-out section, pin the pattern to the floral fabric and cut out. Using the pocket pattern G in the pull-out section, pin the pattern to the contrast floral fabric, then cut out. Using the stripe fabric, cut out two 6.5 x 76cm (2¹⁄₂ x 30¹⁄₂in) strips for the frill. Machine stitch the strips together to make one long piece. Zigzag stitch or trim the seam allowances with pinking shears to stop the edges fraying. Make a DOUBLE HEM along one long edge of the fabric strip, as described on page 114, turning under 5mm (¹⁄₄in) each time.

2. GATHER the frill to 65cm (26in) by hand or machine along one long edge, as described on pages 114–115. With right sides together, aligning the raw edges, lay the frill along the curved edge of the apron skirt. Pin, tack and machine stitch in place. Zigzag stitch or trim along the seam allowances with pinking shears to stop the edges fraying.

3. Bind the top raw edge of the apron bib with an 18cm (7¹⁄₄in) length of bias binding, as described in BINDING AN EDGE on page 112. Trim the ends so they follow the diagonal line of the bib's edges.

4.

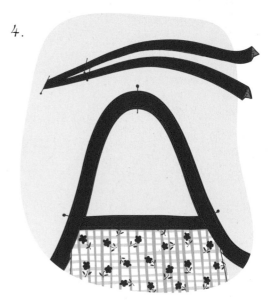

For the 'all-in-one' neck strap/waist ties, fold over an 185cm (74in) length of bias binding along its length, gently steam-pressing as you fold. Fold the binding in half and mark the centre point with a pin. Measure 20cm (8in) out from each side of the centre point, mark these points with pins. Align the top bound edge of the bib with the two pins at either side of the centre point pin. At these points, insert the top corners of the apron bib into the folded binding and re-pin.

5.

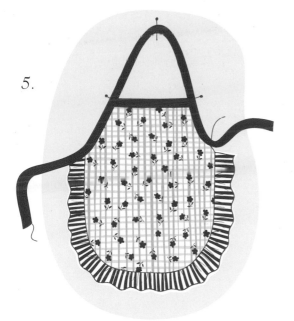

Neatly insert the remaining edges of the bib on the left and right sides, as well as the ends of the frill, into the folded binding. Pin and tack along the whole length of the binding. In one action, machine stitch the apron in place and close the binding. Overlap and stitch the ends of the waist ties to finish.

6.

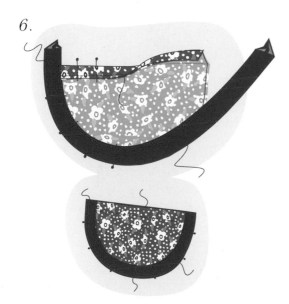

Make a DOUBLE HEM along the upper edge of the pocket, turning under 1.5cm (⁵⁄₈in) each time. Bind the curved edge of the pocket with bias binding, as described in BINDING AN EDGE on page 112, maintaining the curved shape. Topstitch the pocket to the apron, ensuring the ends of the binding are neatly tucked under. Reinforce the top of the pocket with additional stitches and run a vertical line of topstitching through the centre of the pocket to create two separate pouches.

Venetian Vacation

This racier version of Gypsy Spirit is an ode to 'Harry's Bar', with its bold vintage print of gondoliers gliding past a 'Day-Glo' Piazza San Marco. The plunging neck and brief hemline are guaranteed to flatter the curves of even the most weight-challenged spaghetti lover.

You will need:

65cm (26in) length of 90cm (36in) wide conversational print fabric for apron and pocket

15cm (6in) length of 112cm (45in) wide spot print fabric for frill

565cm (226in) length of 2.5cm (1in) bias binding

Sewing machine

Needle and matching sewing thread

Take 1.5cm (⁵/₈in) seam allowances throughout unless otherwise stated

1.

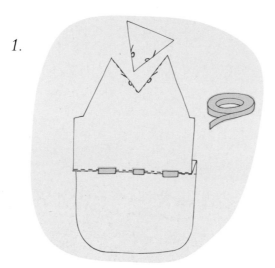

Using apron pattern D in the pull-out section, cut away the V-shaped neckline following the dotted line carefully. Shorten the apron by matching up the dotted lines running across the pattern. Pin the apron to the printed fabric and cut out.

2.

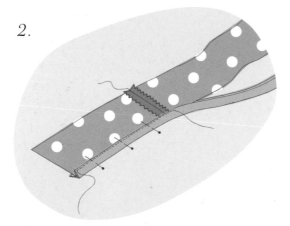

Cut out two 6.5 x 100cm (2¹/₂ x 40in) strips in spotted fabric for the frill. Machine stitch the strips together to make one long piece. Zigzag stitch or trim the seam allowances with pinking shears to stop the edges fraying. Fold a 200cm (80in) length of bias binding over lengthways, gently steam-pressing as you fold. Bind the raw edge of the whole length of the frill as described in BINDING AN EDGE on page 112.

3. Following the instructions for GATHERING – BY HAND on page 114, work a line of running stitches about 1cm (³/₈in) in from the raw edge along the length of the frill and gather it to 112cm (45in). Secure with a few stitches at the end. With right sides together, aligning the raw edges, lay the frill along the curved apron skirt. Pin, tack and machine stitch in place. Zigzag stitch or trim along the seam allowances with pinking shears to stop the edges fraying.

4. Reinforce the V-neck with a short, double row of machine stitches, 12mm (¹/₂in) in from the raw edge. Snip into the point of the V, ensuring you do not cut into the stitched line. Straighten out the V by pulling open the snipped corner and insert the edge into a folded, 36cm (14¹/₄in) length of bias binding. Pin, tack and machine stitch the binding in place, ensuring that it covers the reinforcing stitches. Match up the sides of the V-neck by folding the apron in half lengthways right sides together, and with small machine stitches sew across the folded binding at the centre point (see diagrams for pocket at Step 9) to create a mitre join. Open out the apron and steam-press the V-neck flat.

5. For the 'all-in-one' neck strap/waist ties, fold over a 300cm (120in) length of bias binding lengthways, gently steam-pressing as you fold. Fold the binding in half and mark the centre point with a pin. Measuring 34cm (13¹/₂in) out from each side of the centre point, mark these two positions with pins.

6. To attach the neck strap/waist ties to the apron, align the ends of the V-neck with the two pins at either side of the centre point pin. At these points, insert the ends of the V-neck into the folded binding and re-pin. Trim off the top corners of the apron skirt so they follow the diagonal line of the bib, then neatly insert the remaining edges of the left and right bib and frill into the folded binding. Pin and tack along the whole length of the binding, and in one action machine stitch the apron in place and close the binding. Overlap and stitch the ends of the waist ties to finish.

7. Using the remaining fabric, cut out a 20cm (8in) square for the patch pocket. Fold the pocket in half lengthways and cut out a triangle by cutting in a diagonal line from the top outer corner to the centre fold 6cm (2¼in) down from the top edge. Round off the bottom left- and right-hand corners of the pocket with a 14.5cm (5¾in) diameter plate.

8. Reinforce the V-shaped top edge of the pocket with a short, double row of machine stitches, 12mm (½in) in from the raw edge. Snip into the point of the V, ensuring you do not cut into the stitched line.

9.

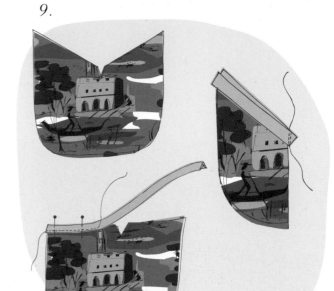

Straighten out the V by pulling open the snipped corner and insert the edge into a folded 26cm (10¼in) length of bias binding. Pin, tack and machine stitch the binding in place, ensuring that it covers the reinforcing stitches. Match up the sides of the V by folding the pocket in half lengthways right sides together, and with small machine stitches sew across the folded binding at the centre point to create a mitre join.

10. To prepare the pocket for attachment to the apron, follow the steps described in PATCH POCKETS – CONTOUR STITCHED on page 116, taking a 1.5cm (⅝in) seam allowance. Pin and tack the pocket to the apron, ensuring that any leftover binding is neatly tucked under the pocket. Sink machine stitches through both pocket and apron layers as close as possible to the folded edge.

Tutti-Frutti

Although simple in design, the V-shaped neckline makes this apron incredibly feminine. The vibrant lemon, orange and watermelon satin bindings add zest to the mouth-watering fruit cocktail print. Serve ice-cream sundaes, smoothies or an exotic fruit punch in this delightful cover-up and you'll receive oohs and aahs of delight.

You will need:

80cm (32in) length of 112cm (45in) wide print fabric for apron

140cm (56in) length of 2cm (7/8in) watermelon bias binding

300cm (120in) length of 2cm (7/8in) orange bias binding

36cm (14 1/4in) length of 2cm (7/8in) lemon bias binding

Sewing machine

Needle and matching sewing thread

1. Using apron pattern D in the pull-out section, cut away the V-shaped neckline, following the dotted line very carefully.

2. Pin the apron pattern to the printed fabric and cut out the shape.

3.

Reinforce the base of the V-neck with a short, double row of machine stitches, 12mm (1/2in) in from the raw edge.

4.

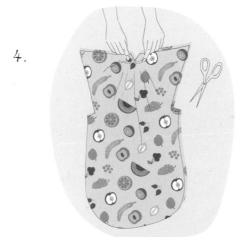

Snip into the point of the V, ensuring you do not cut into the stitched line. Straighten out the V by pulling open the snipped corner.

5.

Following the instructions for BINDING AN EDGE on page 112, bind the edge of the straightened V neckline with a 36cm (14$\frac{1}{4}$in) length of lemon bias binding, ensuring the binding covers the reinforcing stitches.

6.

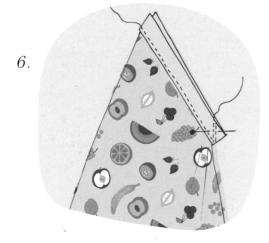

Match up the sides of the V-neck by folding the apron in half lengthways right sides together, and with small machine stitches sew across the folded binding at the centre point to create a mitre.

7.

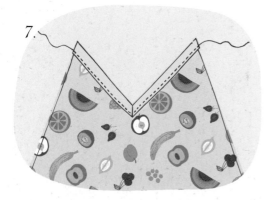

Open out the apron and steam-press the V-neck binding flat.

8. Fold a 140cm (56in) length of watermelon bias binding over lengthways, gently steam-pressing as you fold. Neatly insert the raw edge of the apron skirt into the folded binding. Pin, tack and machine stitch in place.

9. For the 'all-in-one' neck strap/waist ties, fold over a 300cm (120in) length of orange bias binding lengthways, gently steam-pressing as you fold. Fold the binding in half and mark the centre point with a pin. Measuring 34cm (13$\frac{1}{2}$in) out from each side of the centre point, mark these two positions with pins as well.

10. To attach the neck strap/waist ties to the apron, align the ends of the V-neck with the two pins at either side of the centre point pin. At these points, insert the ends of the V-neck into the folded binding and re-pin.

11.

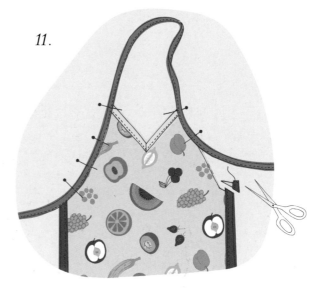

Neatly insert the remaining edges of the left and right bib into the folded binding, trimming off the top corners of the apron skirt so they follow the diagonal line of the bib. Pin and tack along the whole length of the binding, and in one action machine stitch the apron in place and close the binding. Overlap and stitch the ends of the waist ties to finish.

Hawaiian Tropic

This apron is recycled from a vintage tourist shirt, no doubt someone's sentimental souvenir from a trip to Hawaii. This humble, ready-to-wear garment was completely unpicked and its fabric used to make a piece of (kitchen) couture! How cool, and kind, is that? The unusual handkerchief – or should I say, more appropriately, tablecloth-shaped apron skirt – is edged with a frill in a jaunty candy stripe that picks out colours featured in the splashy conversational print of an exotic, palm tree-scattered island vista.

You will need:

Vintage tourist shirt (Size XL) for apron, bib and pocket

20cm (8in) length of 150cm (60in) wide candy stripe fabric for frill

310cm (124in) length of 2.5cm (1in) wide bias binding for waistband/waist ties, bib and neck ties

Pattern paper

Sewing machine

Needle and matching sewing threads

Take 1.5cm (⅝in) seam allowances throughout unless otherwise stated

1. To make the apron pattern, cut out a 46cm (18½in) square of pattern paper. Measure 18cm (7¼in) along both sides from one corner. With a pencil and ruler, draw a straight line to connect the points and cut along it to remove the corner.

2. To make the tapered bib pattern, cut out a 25cm (10in) square of pattern paper. Taking one of the sides as the top edge of the bib, measure in 2.5cm (1in) at both ends. From each of these points, draw a line down to the corresponding corners at the bottom. Cut along each line to taper the pattern piece at each side.

3. Lay the two apron pattern pieces onto your fabric. Pin and cut out.

4. For the frill, cut out two 9 x 150cm (3½ x 60in) strips in candy stripe fabric and machine stitch together to make one long piece. Zigzag stitch or trim the seam allowances with pinking shears to stop the edges fraying. DOUBLE HEM one long edge, as described on page 114, turning under 6mm (¼in) and then 9mm (⅜in), and follow the instructions for GATHERING – BY HAND on page 114 to gather the frill to 142cm (57in).

5.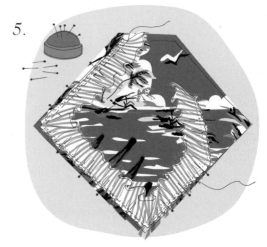

With right sides together, align the raw edge of the frill with the edges of the apron. Pin, tack and machine stitch the frill in place. Remove the running stitches.

6.

Using pocket pattern 5 on page 126, pin the pattern to the fabric and cut out. DOUBLE HEM the top, turning under 2cm (⅞in) each time. Continue by following the instructions for PATCH POCKETS – USING A TEMPLATE on page 116. Pin, tack and machine stitch the finished pocket to the apron.

7. To assemble the apron bib, cut a 20cm (8in) length of bias binding and bind the top edge as described in BINDING AN EDGE on page 112, trimming the ends so they follow the line of the bib sides. For the neck ties, cut two 70cm (28in) lengths of bias binding and neatly insert the left and right sides of the bib into the folded binding. Pin and tack along the whole length of the bindings and close with machine stitches, overlapping the ends to finish.

8.

With wrong sides together and aligning the raw edges, lay the bib onto the apron. Pin, tack and machine stitch together, 5mm (¼in) in from the edge. To make the 'all-in-one' waistband/waist ties, cut a 150cm (60in) length of bias binding, fold it in half and mark the centre point with a pin. Neatly insert the edges of the bib and apron into the folded binding, ensuring the pin is at the centre front of the apron. Pin and tack the open edges along the length of the binding, then machine stitch along the whole length of the binding, attaching the waistband to the bib and apron and closing the binding in one action. Finish by overlapping and stitching the ends of the waist ties.

Petal Power

This '40s tea frock' floral against a dark background is dramatically set off by a wide, petal-shaped border in orange chambray. The dainty pocket is shaped to echo the neat, scalloped edge of the apron, while the nipped-in waist is emphasized by the flattering, full skirt effect created by multiple pleats. Although visually striking, the apron maintains its charm through feminine detailing and a soft, rounded silhouette.

You will need:

85cm (34in) length of 112cm (45in) wide floral print fabric for apron panel and waist ties

50cm (20in) length of 112cm (45in) wide plain fabric for apron border, waistband and pocket

Sewing machine

Needle and matching sewing threads

Take 1.5cm (⅝in) seam allowances throughout unless otherwise stated

1.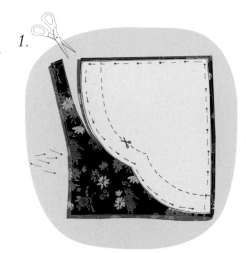

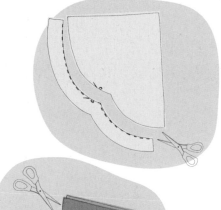

Using apron pattern B in the pull-out section, pin the pattern to the folded floral print fabric and cut out. Un-pin the paper pattern, lay it on your work surface and following the dotted line, cut away the scalloped border section. Pin just the border paper pattern to the folded plain fabric and cut out.

2.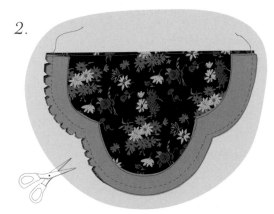

With the right side of the border strip facing the wrong side of the apron piece, pin the scalloped border strip to the apron. Tack and machine stitch together. Trim down the seam allowances, cutting out wedge shapes along the curved edges.

3.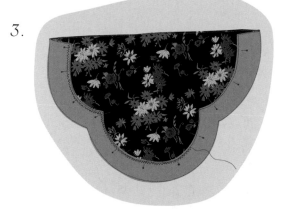

Turn the scalloped hem border strip to the right side of the apron and steam-press flat. Secure the raw edge of the border strip to the apron with pins. Tack and machine topstitch 5mm (¼in) in along the edge. Go over the topstitching with a wide zigzag stitch, so that the raw edge of the scalloped border strip is completely covered.

4.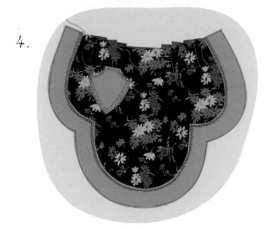

Using pocket pattern 7 on page 122, pin the pattern to the remaining plain fabric and cut out two pocket pieces. To assemble the pocket, follow the steps in PATCH POCKETS – BAGGED-OUT on page 115, using a 1cm (3/8in) seam allowance. Attach the finished pocket to the apron. Make three 2cm (7/8in) deep pleats at each end of the top of the apron, securing with machine stitches 12mm (1/2in) in from the raw edge.

5. To make the waist ties, cut out two 17 x 70cm (6³/₄ x 28in) strips of floral print fabric and follow the steps described in WAIST TIES – QUICK 'N' EASY on page 119.

6. Cut out a 13 x 43cm (5¹/₄ x 17in) strip of plain fabric for the waistband and follow the steps in WAISTBAND – WITH WAIST TIES on page 119 to finish.

Raspberry Ruffle

A shower of leafy sprigs and flower buds provides a pretty backdrop for this delightful display of rococo-inspired ruffles that give this apron its playful and coquettish quality. The narrow central ruffle is worked in a flattering chevron pattern, while the deeper flounce at the hem adds weight to the apron skirt.

You will need:

80cm (32in) length of 90cm (36in) wide floral print fabric for apron, pocket and waist ties

45cm (18in) length of 112cm (46in) wide plain fabric for waistband and ruffles

Sewing machine

Needle and matching sewing thread

Take 1.5cm (⁵⁄₈in) seam allowances throughout unless otherwise stated

Note:

To speed things up, you could replace the double-hemmed ruffles with wide ribbon. However, take the time to cut out the pocket piece carefully so that the pattern matches the apron and does not detract from the overall effect.

1.

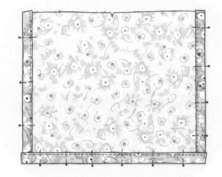

Cut out a 51 x 68cm (20¹⁄₂ x 27in) rectangle for the apron in the floral fabric. Make a DOUBLE HEM along both short sides and the bottom edge, as described on page 114, turning under 1.5cm (⁵⁄₈in) each time.

2.

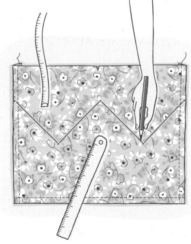

Lay the apron right side up on your work surface. To draw the zigzag pattern for the narrow ruffle appliqué, measure 13.5cm (5¹⁄₄in) down from the top raw edge along both sides and mark the points with a fine, felt-tip pen. Make another mark 13.5cm (5¹⁄₄in) down from the top edge along the centre front. Measure 22cm (8³⁄₄in) up from the hem and 15.5cm (6¹⁄₄in) across from the left-hand side of the panel and mark the spot with the pen. Repeat for the right-hand side of the apron. Join the five dots using the straight edge of a ruler.

3. Cut out two 13 x 65cm (5¹⁄₄ x 26in) strips in plain fabric for the wide ruffle, machine stitch together to make one long strip and DOUBLE HEM all four sides, turning under by 6mm (¹⁄₄in) and then by 9mm (³⁄₈in). Sew running stitches along the whole length of the strip, 3cm (1¹⁄₄in) down from the top edge, and GATHER the fabric, as described in GATHERING – BY HAND on page 144, to a length of 62cm (24³⁄₄in).

4.

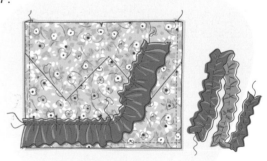

Aligning the bottom edge of the ruffle with the apron hem, pin, tack and machine stitch the ruffle in place. Remove the running stitches.

5. Cut out two 9 x 83cm (3¹⁄₂ x 33¹⁄₄in) strips in plain fabric for the narrow ruffle, machine stitch together to make one long strip and DOUBLE HEM along all four sides, turning under by 6mm (¹⁄₄in) and then by 9mm (³⁄₈in). Sew running stitches along the whole length of the strip, 3cm (1¹⁄₄in) down from the top edge and gather the fabric, as described in GATHERING – BY HAND, to a length of 80cm (32in).

6. Pin the narrow ruffle to the apron, carefully aligning the running stitches with the drawn zigzag pattern. Tack and machine stitch in place. Remove the running stitches.

7.

Using pocket pattern 5, pin the pattern to the fabric and cut out. DOUBLE HEM the top, turning under 2cm (⁷/₈in) each time. Continue by following the instructions for PATCH POCKETS – USING A TEMPLATE on page 116. Pin, tack and machine stitch the finished pocket to the apron. Take a needle and thread, and work a line of running stitches along the top raw edge of the apron. Gently pull the thread to GATHER the fabric to 44cm (17¹/₂in).

8. Cut out two 13 x 73cm (5¹/₄ x 29in) strips of floral print fabric for the waist ties. DOUBLE HEM the long edges by folding over by 6mm (¹/₄in) and then by 9mm (³/₈in). Pin, tack and machine stitch in place, stitching as close as possible to the folded edges. Repeat this process for one short end of each waist tie. Concertina-fold into three equal parts the unhemmed ends of both waist ties and machine stitch in place. Put them to one side.

9. Cut out a 13 x 47cm (5¹/₄ x 18in) strip of plain fabric for the waistband and follow steps 1, 2 and 3, as described in WAISTBAND – BASIC on page 117.

10. Open out the folded waistband and align the raw ends of the waist ties with the ends of the front side of the waistband, ensuring the top edge of the ties lies just below the crease. Pin, tack and stitch in place. Continue with WAISTBAND – BASIC steps 4 and 5.

Truly Scrumptious (page 66)

Calico Kitty (page 68)

Sweetheart (page 70)

Domestic Diva (page 62)

Busy Lizzie (page 60)

Prairie Rose (page 58)

chapter 4

Kitsch 'n' Cute

Prairie Rose

Indigo chambray and honest-to-goodness gingham provide a look with whimsical, American Western charm. So wave goodbye to dressing dilemmas and wardrobe crises when it comes to choosing attire for barbecuing those T-bone steaks. Guaranteed come summertime, you'll be the only non-Calamity Jane on the block. Look out for bold, overblown floral prints to cut up and use for the appliqués.

You will need:

50cm (20in) length of 112cm (45in) wide chambray fabric for the apron and waistband

50cm (20in) length of 112cm (45in) wide gingham fabric for the frill and ties

25cm (4in) length of 110cm (44in) wide floral print fabric for the appliqués

270cm (108in) length of 12mm (¹/₂in) wide bias binding

25cm (10in) BONDAWEB® (iron-on double-sided appliqué adhesive)

Sewing machine

Needle and matching sewing threads

Take 1.5cm (⁵/₈in) seam allowances throughout unless otherwise stated

Note:

A pair of sharp embroidery scissors is essential to cut neatly around the floral motifs with ease.

1.

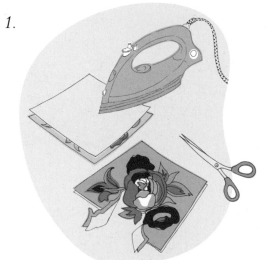

Using apron pattern A in the pull-out section and pocket pattern 3 on page 122, pin both patterns to the chambray fabric and cut out. To make the floral appliqués, choose suitable motifs on the floral fabric. Follow the steps for APPLIQUÉ on page 112.

2. Cut out three 6 x 77cm (2¹/₂ x 31in) strips of gingham fabric for the frill. Machine stitch together to make one long piece. Zigzag stitch or trim the seam allowances with pinking shears to stop the edges fraying. Bind one long edge of the fabric strip with a 225cm (90in) length of bias binding, as described in BINDING AN EDGE on page 112.

3.

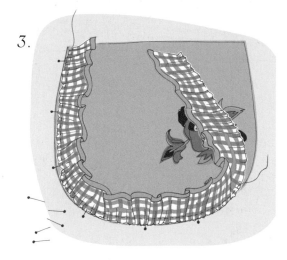

Gather the fabric strip to 125cm (50in) in length by hand or machine, as described in GATHERING – BY HAND on page 114 or GATHERING – BY MACHINE on page 115. With right sides together, aligning the raw edges, lay the frill along the apron's curved edge. Pin, tack and machine stitch in place.

4.

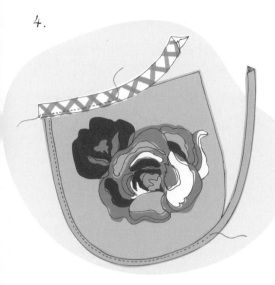

Bind the shaped edge of the pocket with a 38cm (15in) length of bias binding. Cut out a 3 x 18cm ($1^1/_4$ x 7in) strip of gingham fabric diagonally on the bias. Fold both long edges over 5mm ($^1/_4$in) and press. Aligning the folded edges, re-fold in half and press. Bind the top edge of the pocket with the gingham strip. Pin and stitch the pocket to the apron – ensuring the ends of the binding are neatly tucked under the pocket – carefully topstitching over the existing stitches on the binding.

5. Cut out a 15 x 49cm (6 x $19^1/_2$in) rectangle in the chambray fabric for the waistband and two 9 x 48cm ($3^1/_2$ x 19) strips in gingham for the ties.

6. Following the instructions for GATHERING – BY HAND, work a short line of running stitches about 12mm ($^1/_2$in) in from the raw edge at the centre waist of the apron. Gather the waist measurement from 55cm (22in) to 46cm ($18^1/_2$in), including the frills. Make the waistband as described in WAISTBAND – WITH WAIST TIES on page 119.

Busy Lizzie

This apron could have slipped right off the page of a 50s housekeeping magazine. It's fun, flirty, feminine and 'happy homemaker' through and through. And in lipstick pink, what could be more 50s? The oversized flower head appliqué doubles as a pocket, while the waist ties form a frivolous 'pussy cat' bow at the back.

You will need:

65cm (26in) length of 112cm (45in) wide plain fabric for apron, waistband and ties

25cm (10in) length of 136cm (54in) wide floral print fabric for apron frill and pocket

85cm (34in) length of 112cm (45in) wide plain fabric for pocket frill

125cm (50in) length of jumbo rickrack in tonal colour

100cm (40in) length of rickrack in tonal colour

Sewing machine

Needle and matching sewing thread

Take 1.5cm (⁵/₈in) seam allowances throughout unless otherwise stated

1. Using apron pattern A in the pull-out section, pin the pattern to the fabric and cut out. From the remaining fabric, cut out a 15 x 49cm (6 x 19¹/₂in) strip for the waistband and another two 13 x 63cm (5¹/₄ x 25¹/₄in) strips for the two waist ties.

2.

Cut out three 7.5 x 77cm (3 x 31in) strips for the apron frill. Using pocket pattern 10 on page 121, cut out two pockets from the floral print fabric. Machine stitch the strips together to make one long piece and zigzag stitch or pink the selvedge. Make a DOUBLE HEM, as described on page 114, along one long edge of the fabric strip, turning under 7mm (¹/₃in) and then 8mm (³/₈in), and stitch in place. Gather the other long edge to 125cm (50in) by hand or machine, as described in GATHERING – BY HAND on page 114 or GATHERING – BY MACHINE on page 115. With right sides together, aligning raw edges, lay the frill along the apron edge. Pin, tack and machine stitch in place. Stitch a 125cm (50in) length of jumbo rickrack over the seam where the apron and frill join.

3.

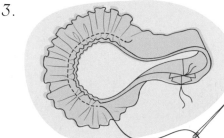

To make the pocket frill, cut out a 9 x 83cm (3¹/₂ x 33in) strip in plain fabric. With right sides together, machine stitch the two short ends to make a loop and press the seam allowances flat. With wrong sides together, align the raw edges and fold the loop in half lengthways. Steam-press flat. GATHER the fabric into a flat ring, 48cm (19in) in circumference.

4.

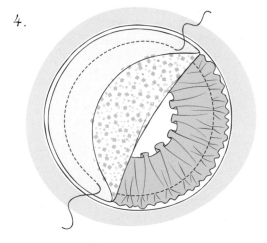

With one pocket piece right side up, lay the ring on top with the frill side facing inwards and the raw edge facing outwards and aligned with the raw edge of the circle. Pin, tack and machine stitch around the circle. Place the other pocket piece, right side down, on top of the frill. Follow the steps for PATCH POCKETS – BAGGED-OUT on page 115, stitching through all the layers, following the original stitch line but leaving a 6cm (2¹/₄in) opening in the stitching.

5. Machine stitch a 50cm (20in) length of rickrack for the flower stalk and two 25cm (10in) lengths for the leaves onto the apron front, as in the photographs. Position pocket at the top of the stalk and stitch around the seam where the pocket joins the frill. Leave a 15cm (6in) gap at the top for the opening.

6. GATHER the top of the apron to 46cm (18¼in). Attach the waistband as in WAISTBAND – BASIC on page 117. Make ties as in WAIST TIES – QUICK 'N' EASY on page 119. Concertina-fold the unhemmed end into three equal parts and pin on the right side of the waistband, with raw edges aligned. Stitch vertically, trim selvedge, then fold the waist tie back on itself and stitch again, hiding the selvedge. Repeat on the other side of the waistband.

Domestic Diva

Whimsical appliqués in vintage cotton dress fabrics evoke quaint retro homewares, while the folded edges of the gingham panel running across the front provide a 3-D tablecloth effect. This apron is not only practical – with its dainty patch pocket for your iPod – it's visually appealing too, positively encouraging you to make a brew. Forget the housework!

You will need:

55cm (22in) length of 112cm (45in) wide plain fabric for apron and waistband

70cm (28in) length of 112cm (45in) wide gingham check fabric for apron panel, pocket and waist ties

Two 20 x 30cm (8 x 12in) pieces of printed fabric for appliqués

30cm (12in) piece of BONDAWEB® (iron-on double-sided appliqué adhesive)

Sewing machine

Needle and matching sewing thread

Take 1.5cm ($^5/_8$in) seam allowances throughout unless otherwise stated

1. Cut out a 52.5 x 68cm (21 x 27in) rectangle for the apron and a 13 x 47cm ($5^1/_4$ x 19in) strip for the waistband in plain fabric. For the apron panel, cut out a 34 x 68cm ($13^1/_2$ x 27in) panel in the gingham check fabric.

2.

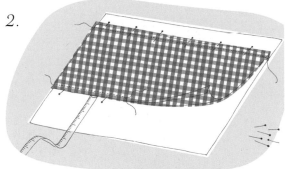

Fold both long edges of the check panel over 1.5cm ($^5/_8$in) to the wrong side and press. Lay the panel on top of the apron, 15cm (6in) above the bottom edge of the apron. Pin, tack and topstitch through the panel and apron layers, 5mm ($^1/_4$in) in from the folded edges.

3.

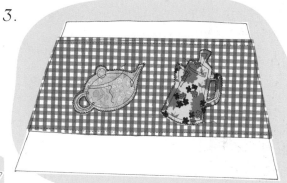

To make the appliqués, trace the teapot and coffee pot templates on pages 125 and 126 onto paper and cut out. Follow the APPLIQUÉ instructions on page 112. Use decorative machine stitches, as shown above, to add an extra dimension to the appliquéd motifs.

4. Make a DOUBLE HEM along both short edges and the bottom edge of the apron, as described on page 114, folding over to the wrong side by 1.5cm ($^5/_8$in) and then by another 1.5cm ($^5/_8$in).

5. GATHER the top edge of the apron to 44cm (17$\frac{1}{2}$in) by hand or machine, as described on pages 114–115. Make sure the gathers are even across the whole width of the apron.

6.

Make the waistband as described in WAISTBAND – BASIC on page 117. To make the waist ties, cut out two 13 x 63cm (5$\frac{1}{4}$ x 25in) strips of check fabric. Make a DOUBLE HEM along both long edges and one short edge, folding over by 7mm ($\frac{1}{3}$in) and then by 8mm ($\frac{3}{8}$in). Concertina-fold the unhemmed end into three equal parts and pin at one end on the right side of the waistband, with raw edges aligned. Stitch vertically in place, trim the selvedge, then fold the waist tie back on itself and machine stitch again, making sure the selvedge is hidden. Repeat with the remaining waist tie on the other side of the waistband.

7.

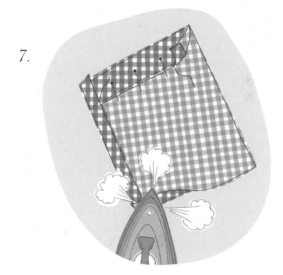

To make the little patch pocket, cut out a 13 x 16cm (5$\frac{1}{4}$ x 6$\frac{1}{2}$in) piece from the remaining check fabric. Make a DOUBLE HEM on one short edge, folding over by 1.5cm ($\frac{5}{8}$in) and then by 3cm (1$\frac{1}{4}$in) to the wrong side. Fold the three remaining edges over by 1.5cm ($\frac{5}{8}$in) to the wrong side and press. Pin and tack the pocket to the check panel, ensuring the top edges are aligned, and topstitch in place.

Truly Scrumptious

This cute little confection is good enough to eat and will certainly appeal to fondant fanciers everywhere. The mouth-watering cupcake appliqué is very easy to assemble and so, too, the whimsical muffin case, which also functions as a roomy pouch pocket to hold the accoutrements of the novice pastry chef. Satisfy your sweet tooth with some fun food!

You will need:

35cm (14in) length of 110cm (44in) wide plain fabric for apron

28 x 28cm (11 x 11in) piece of stripe fabric for pocket

24 x 24cm (9¹/₂ x 9¹/₂in) piece of plain fabric for cupcake appliqué

10 x 20cm (4 x 8in) piece of plain fabric for frosting appliqué

Small piece of fabric for cherry appliqué

2 x 24cm (9¹/₂in) lengths of jumbo rickrack in contrasting colours

275cm (110in) length of 2cm (⁷/₈in) wide bias binding

25cm (10in) BONDAWEB® (iron-on double-sided appliqué adhesive)

Sewing machine

Needle and matching sewing thread

Take 1.5cm (⁵/₈in) seam allowances throughout unless otherwise stated

1. Using apron pattern G in the pull-out section, pin the pattern to the plain fabric and carefully cut out the apron shape.

2.

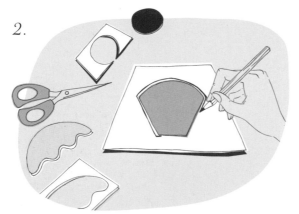

To make the appliqué, trace the cupcake, frosting and cherry templates on page 124 onto paper and cut out. Follow the APPLIQUÉ instructions on page 112.

3.

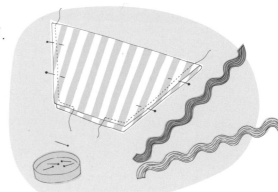

To make the pocket, fold the striped fabric in half with right sides together so the stripes run vertically. Using pocket pattern 9 on page 124, pin to the fabric. Cut the pocket out. Taking a 1cm (³/₈in) seam allowance, follow the steps for PATCH POCKETS – BAGGED-OUT on page 115. Machine stitch a 24cm (9¹/₂in) and a 22cm (8³/₄in) length of jumbo rickrack across the patch pocket, ensuring the ends are neatly tucked under. Lay the pocket over the cupcake appliqué, then pin, tack and machine stitch through the pocket and apron layers along the sides and bottom, as close as possible to the edge. Reinforce the top corners of the pocket with additional stitches.

4. Bind the top raw edge of the apron bib with an 18cm (7¼in) length of bias binding as described in BINDING AN EDGE on page 112. Trim the ends so they follow the diagonal line of the bib's sides. Bind the raw edge of the apron skirt with a 70cm (28in) length of bias binding and trim off any excess.

5. For the 'all-in-one' neck strap/waist ties, fold an 185cm (74in) length of bias binding, gently steam-pressing as you fold. Fold the binding in half and mark the centre point with a pin. Measure 20cm (8in) out from each side of the centre point and mark these points with pins. Align the top bound edge of the bib with the two pins at either side of the centre point pin. At these points, insert the top corners of the apron bib into the folded binding and re-pin.

6.

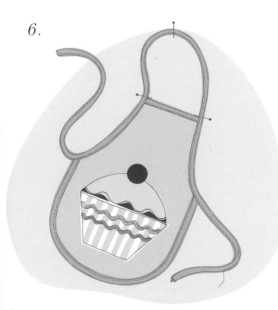

Neatly insert the remaining edges of the bib on the left and right sides into the folded binding. Pin and tack along the whole length of the binding. In one action, machine stitch the apron in place and close the binding. Overlap and stitch the ends of the waist ties to finish.

Calico Kitty

This bib-style cover-up is made from tenugui – a traditional Japanese hand-dyed cotton used as a hand towel or handkerchief. The word literally means 'to wipe one's hands'. During the Edo period it was used for bandage, to tie Japanese sandals and as a headscarf. The funky feline appliqué is made from toile de Jouy, another textile with a long history. The dark blues are enlivened with a bright turquoise binding. A purr-fect companion for any child at dinnertime.

You will need:

35 x 50cm (14 x 20in) piece of fish print fabric for bib

20 x 80cm (8 x 32in) piece of contrast floral print fabric for appliqué and waist ties

220cm (88in) length of 2cm ($^7/_8$in) wide bias binding

25cm (10in) BONDAWEB® (iron-on double-sided appliqué adhesive)

Scraps of pink and blue felt

1 button

Sewing machine

Needle and matching sewing threads

Note:

It is easier to bind the bib if the fabric is slightly stiff. Choose a medium-weight cotton canvas, or back light-weight fabric with canvas by bonding the two pieces together with iron-on double-sided appliqué adhesive before cutting out.

1. Using apron pattern F in the pull-out section, pin the pattern to the fish print fabric and cut out.

2.

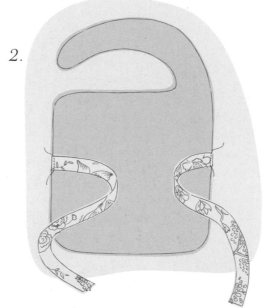

For the waist ties, cut out two 7 x 50cm ($2^3/_4$ x 20in) strips from the contrast floral fabric. With right sides together, fold in half lengthways and machine stitch both strips along their one short end and along the length of the strips. Trim the corners, turn the ties right side out and press. Aligning the raw ends of the ties with the raw edges on each side of the bib's wrong side, machine stitch 5mm ($^1/_4$in) in from the edge.

3.

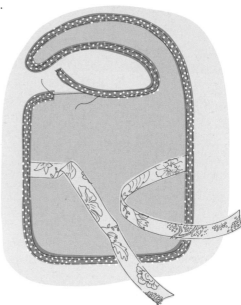

Bind the raw edges of the bib with a 190cm (76in) length of bias binding, as described in BINDING AN EDGE on page 112. Ensure the end of the binding is neatly tucked under.

4. To make the kitten appliqué, trace the template on page 123 onto paper and cut out. Follow the APPLIQUÉ instructions on page 112.

5.

Cut out the eyes and nose in felt, and hand stitch in place. Add the whiskers with a straight machine stitch worked back and forth. For the bow at the neck, use the 30cm (12in) length of leftover binding and follow the instructions for Bows – Crisscross on page 113.

6.

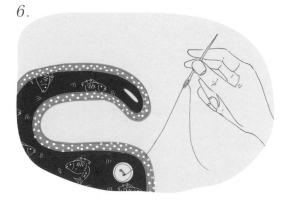

Make a buttonhole at the end of the shoulder strap and attach a button to secure. Alternatively, you could attach two small squares of VELCRO®.

Sweetheart

This frilly heart-shaped bib will send his pulse racing. Perfect with heels — the daintier and
higher the better! In pretty pink and white gingham, it's as soft and sweet as marshmallow.
Satin ribbon at the neck adds a decadent lingerie touch. This style is pure, unadulterated,
50s 'chocolate box' glamour.

You will need:

130cm (52in) length
of 112cm (45in) wide
gingham fabric for
apron, heart-shaped
bib, pocket and frills

150cm (60in) length
of 1.5cm (5/8in) wide
satin ribbon for neck
ties

Sewing machine

Needle and matching
sewing threads

Take 1.5cm (5/8in) seam
allowances throughout
unless otherwise stated

1. Using apron pattern E in the pull-out section, pin the pattern to the gingham fabric and cut out.

2. For the apron skirt frill, cut out three 7.5 x 103cm (3 x 40½in) strips of gingham fabric. Machine stitch the strips together to make one long piece. Zigzag stitch or trim the seam allowances with pinking shears to stop the edges fraying. Make a DOUBLE HEM, as described on page 114, turning under by 5mm (¼in) each time, along one long length of the fabric strip. Gather the frill along the other long raw edge to 147cm (58½in), as described in GATHERING — BY MACHINE on page 115.

3.

With right sides together, aligning the raw edges, lay the frill along the curved edge of the apron skirt. Pin, tack and machine stitch in place. Zigzag stitch or trim the seam allowances with pinking shears to stop the edges fraying. GATHER the waist at each end of the apron panel so that the finished width including the frill is 46cm (18½in).

4. For the waistband, cut out a 15 x 49cm (6 x 19½in) rectangle. and for the waist ties cut out two 8 x 48cm (3¼ x 19¼in) strips in gingham fabrics. To assemble, follow the steps described in WAISTBAND — WITH WAIST TIES on page 119.

5. Using pocket pattern 3 on page 122, pin the pattern to the gingham fabric and cut out two pocket shapes. Taking a 1.5cm (5/8in) seam allowance, follow the steps described in PATCH POCKETS — BAGGED-OUT on page 115. Pin, tack and stitch the pocket to the apron.

6. To make the heart-shaped bib, pin bib pattern I in the pull-out section to a double layer of the remaining gingham fabric and cut out.

7.

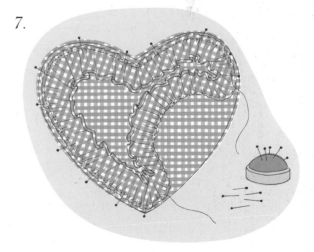

To make the bib frill, join two 7.5 x 78cm (3 x 31in) strips to make a loop, DOUBLE HEM, turning under by 5mm (¼in) each time, and GATHER to 86cm (34¼in), as described in GATHERING — BY HAND on page 114.

8.

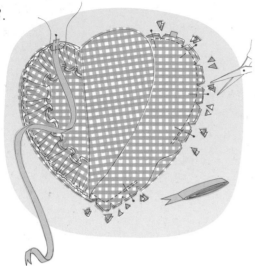

With right sides together, and all raw edges aligned, place the frill all around one of the bib pieces. Pin, tack and machine stitch in place. Cut two 75cm (30in) lengths of satin ribbon and attach one at each end of the bib top edge. With right sides together, lay the other bib piece directly over its twin to sandwich the attached frill and neck ties. Aligning the raw edges, pin, tack and stitch all the way around the sides, remembering to leave a 5cm (2in) gap for bagging out. Trim all the seam allowances, making little wedge-shaped snips in the curved edges so the seams will lie flat. Turn the bib right side out.

9.

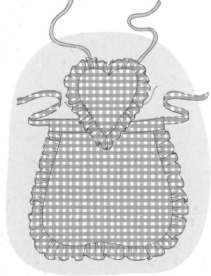

Close the gap with slipstitches, press and topstitch 1cm ($^3/_8$in) in from the seam where bib meets frill. Lay bib over apron, aligning the point of the heart with apron centre front at bottom of waistband.

10. Pin and tack the bib in place. Finish by sinking machine stitching through all the layers between the bib and frill seam.

Butcher's Boy (page 86)

Spring Fever (page 76)

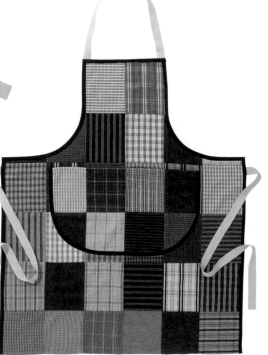

Mood Indigo (page 84)

Safari Style (page 80)

Singapore Sling (page 88)

Pretty Posies (page 78)

chapter 5

Fun & Function

Spring Fever

A neat, contemporary wraparound style – and stylish too! Daffodil yellow and sapling green capture the freshness of spring, and provide the perfect look for gardening pursuits. With its eye-catching, patterned hip band that doubles as a row of pockets for holding garden fork, trowel and twine, this cheeky little apron fuses fashion with function.

You will need:

50cm (20in) length of 92cm (36in) wide woven stripe fabric for the apron

30cm (12in) length of 92cm (36in) floral print fabric for the pocket

350cm (140in) length of 3.5cm (1³/₈in) wide woven tape

Sewing machine

Needle and matching sewing threads

Take 1.5cm (⁵/₈in) seam allowances throughout unless otherwise stated

Note:

Choose a woven stripe for the apron fabric, as the pattern needs to be visible both on the front and the reverse.

1. To make the pocket, cut out a 24.5 x 67cm (9³/₄ x 27in) rectangle of floral fabric. Along one long edge, fold over 1.5cm (⁵/₈in) to the right side and press. Place a 68cm (27in) length of woven tape over the fold so that one edge of the tape is aligned with the edge of the fold. Pin the tape in place, tack and machine stitch onto the fabric as close to both edges as possible.

2. Measure 22cm (8³/₄in) in from one short side of the rectangle and run a line of pins from top to bottom. Repeat on the opposite side.

3.

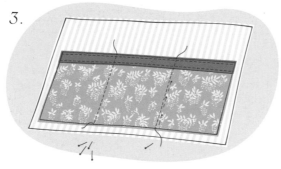

To make the apron, cut out a 40 x 72cm (16 x 29in) rectangle of stripe fabric. Lay it on your work surface right side up and place the floral patterned pocket on top of it, right side up, leaving a 2.5cm (1in) border along one long edge and at both short sides. Machine stitch through both pocket and apron layers along each pinned line.

4.

Fold both short sides of the apron over 1.5cm (⁵/₈in) to the right side and then by another 1.5cm (⁵/₈in), covering the raw side edges of the pocket. Pin, tack and machine stitch in place, stitching as close as possible to the folded edge. Repeat at the apron hem.

5.

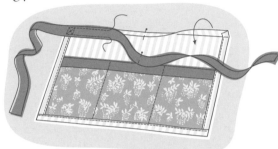

Along the top edge of the apron, fold over 1.5cm (⁵⁄₈in) to the right side and press. Fold the apron in half lengthways and mark the top centre front with a pin. Fold the remaining length of woven tape in half and mark the centre with a pin. Place the tape over the folded edge of the apron, so the pins match up and the top edge of the tape is aligned with the folded edge of the apron. Pin the tape in place, tack and machine stitch to the apron, stitching as close as possible to both edges of the tape.

6.
Reinforce both sides of the waistband where the apron ends by stitching a crisscross box. Overlap and stitch the ends of the waist ties to finish.

Pretty Posies

This charming little apron is a tribute to my grandmother Annie, who owned a wonderful collection of embroidered table linen, painstakingly handcrafted by herself and her three sisters, Nellie, Maggie and Lilly, in the 1930s and 40s. The pouch pockets are cut from a vintage tablecloth – not belonging to Nan, of course, those are far too precious to use – found in a shop selling vintage clothing and homewares.

You will need:

50cm (20in) length of 145cm (58in) wide woven gingham fabric for the apron and ties

Vintage embroidered tablecloth for the pockets

35.5cm (14in) length of 2.5cm (1in) wide bias binding

Sewing machine

Needle and matching sewing thread

Take 1.5cm (⅝in) seam allowances throughout unless otherwise stated

Note:

Choose a woven gingham check for the apron fabric, as the pattern needs to be visible both on the front and the reverse.

1.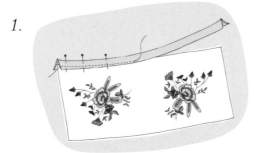

To make the pocket, cut out a 16.5 x 35.5cm (6½ x 14in) rectangle from an embroidered tablecloth, ensuring a floral motif is positioned as close as possible to the centre of each half. Bind the top edge with a 35.5cm (14in) length of bias binding, as described in BINDING AN EDGE on page 112.

2. To make the apron, cut out a 28 x 40.5cm (11 x 16in) rectangle of gingham fabric. Lay it right side up and place the embroidered panel on top, right side up, leaving a 2.5cm (1in) border along the bottom edge and at both sides. Tack the panel to the apron.

3.

Cut out a 2.5 x 19cm (1 x 7½in) strip of gingham fabric. Fold both long sides over 5mm (¼in) to the wrong side and press. Place the gingham strip in the centre of the panel and in between the two embroidered motifs, tucking any excess strip out of sight at the top. Pin, tack and machine stitch in place.

4.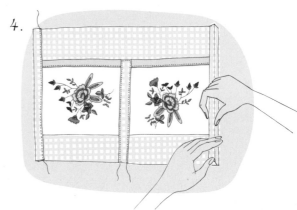

Fold both short sides of the apron over 1.5cm (⅝in) to the right side and then by another 1.5cm (⅝in), covering the raw edges of the pocket. Pin, tack and machine stitch in place. Repeat on the apron hem.

5. Cut out two 8.5 x 103cm (3¼ x 41in) strips of gingham fabric and follow the instructions to make a WAISTBAND – TWO-PIECE/ALL-IN-ONE on page 118.

6.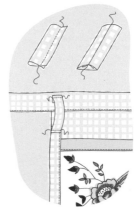

To make the belt loops, cut two 5 x 7.5cm (2 x 3in) strips of gingham fabric. Fold one strip over lengthways, right sides together, and align the raw edges. Taking a 1cm (½in) seam allowance, machine stitch along the full length of the loop. Turn right side out and press. Fold under the raw edges of the loop, line up with the apron side over the waistband and attach with several machine stitches. Repeat for the other belt loop.

Safari Style

In faded desert tones and made from utilitarian calico, linen and cord, this man's apron is more 'Out of Africa' than 'Out of London', where it was made. Inspired by the great outdoors, this style is loosely based on a tarpaulin, or tarp, featuring reinforced eyelets at the corners to form attachment points for the neck strap and waist ties. Replacing the hardwearing materials with pretty ribbons and botanical printed cottons can instantly feminize this style for the lady of the house.

You will need:

75cm (30in) length of 112cm (45in) wide heavyweight calico fabric for apron panel and large pocket

20 x 54cm (8 x 21½in) piece of plain linen fabric in contrast colour for small pocket and reinforcing patches

270cm (108in) length of 2.5cm (1in) wide bias binding in contrast colour

300cm (120in) length of 20mm (⅞in) sash cord

Four 8mm (⅜in) metal eyelets with washers

Pattern paper

Sewing machine

Needle and matching sewing threads

Masking tape

Take 1.5cm (⅝in) seam allowances throughout unless otherwise stated

1.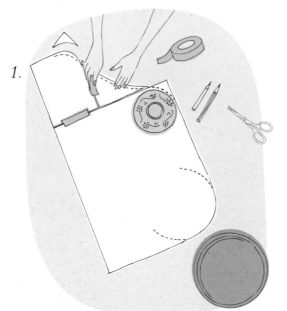

To make the L-shaped apron pattern, draw a 37 x 45cm (14¾ x 18in) rectangle and a 16 x 25cm (6½ x 10in) rectangle on paper and cut out. Place the smaller rectangle with one short edge touching one short edge of the larger rectangle and with one long edge of each in line, to create an L shape with the longest edge measuring 70cm (28in). Stick together with masking tape. Lay the paper pattern piece on your work surface with the bottom edge of the L facing you and place a round tray 30cm (12in) in diameter in the lower right-hand corner so the rim touches both edges of the paper pattern. With a pencil, draw around the tray to round off the corner. Carefully cut along the pencil line and insert this cut-off corner into the angle where the large and small rectangles meet. Stick together with masking tape. Using a bowl 14.5cm (5¾in) in diameter as a template, round off the two upper corners of the bib section and apron using the same method.

2. For the small pocket, cut out a 17 x 19.5cm (6¾ x 7¾in) rectangle in paper and round off the bottom corners with an eggcup. For the large pocket, cut out a 19.5 x 35cm (7¾ x 14in) rectangle in paper and round off the bottom corners with the bowl.

3. Fold the calico fabric in half down its length and pin the apron pattern to it, with the longest edge aligned with the fold, and cut out. Cut out the large pocket from the remaining calico. Cut a 38cm (15¼in) length of bias binding and bind the top edge of the large pocket. Fold over 1.5cm (⅝in) on the remaining three sides of the pocket and pin, tack and stitch in place.

4. Pin the small pocket pattern to the contrast fabric and cut out. Make a DOUBLE HEM at the top edge, as shown on page 114, folding over by 1.5cm (⅝in) to the wrong side each time. Fold under 1.5cm (⅝in) to the wrong side on the remaining three sides and pin, tack and stitch in place.

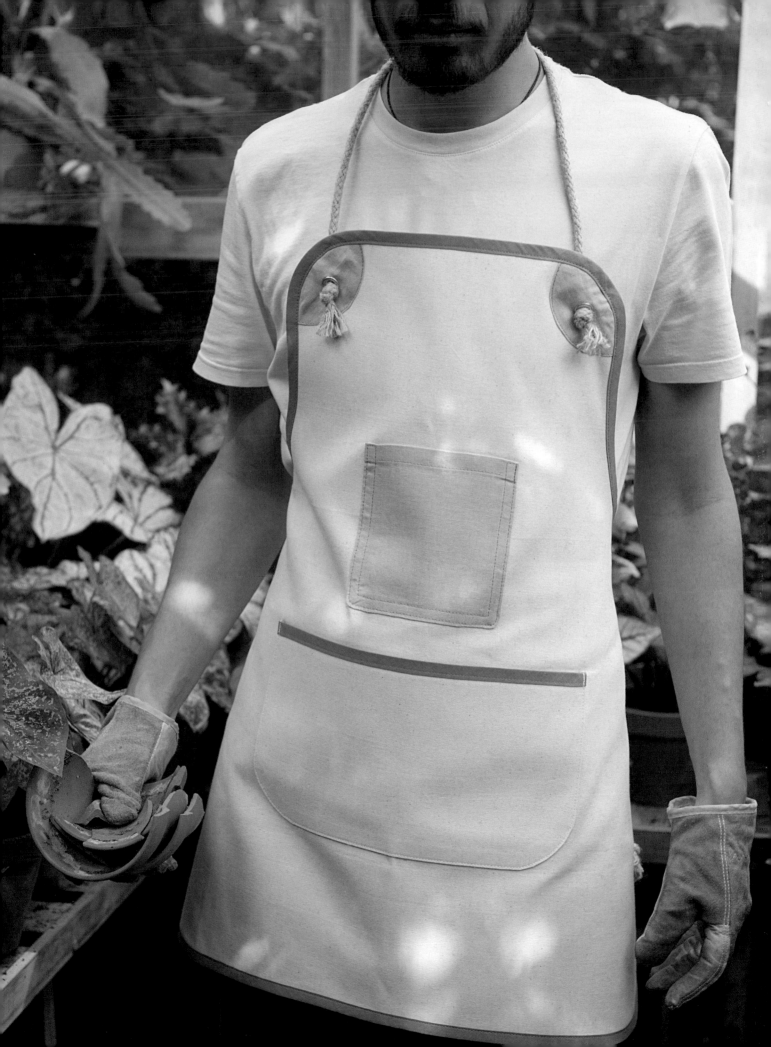

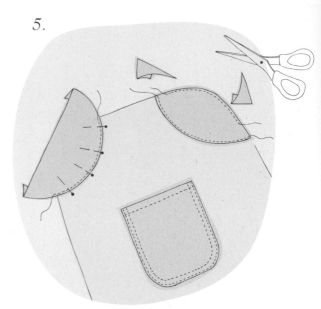

5.

Using the remaining contrast fabric, cut out two circles for the reinforcing patches using the bowl as a template. Fold under 1.5cm ($^5/_8$in) to the wrong side all round the edge of each circle and press, then cut both circles in half. With the right side of the apron facing upwards on your work surface, place a half circle wrong side down over the two upper curved corners of the bib, as indicated, where the neck strap will be attached. Place the other two half circles over the two upper curved corners of the apron, where the waist ties will be attached. Pin, tack and stitch in place. Trim off any excess fabric so that the outer edge of each patch exactly follows the line of each curved corner.

6. Cut a 225cm (90in) length of bias binding and bind the apron edges completely, as described in BINDING AN EDGE on page 112, ensuring the binding covers the raw edges of each patch. Overlap the binding and tuck any excess out of sight.

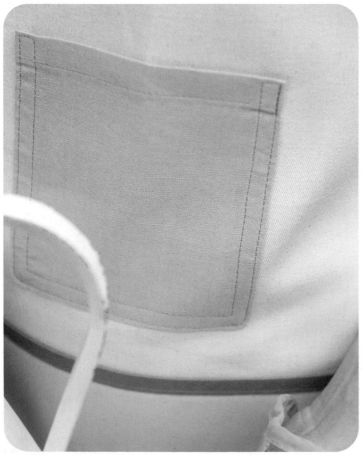

7.

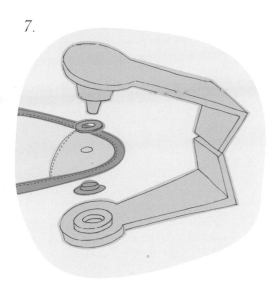

Following the manufacturer's instructions, attach the eyelets to the four upper corners of the apron, through the reinforcing patches.

8.

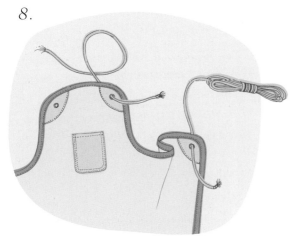

Cut one 70cm (28in) and two 100cm (40in) lengths of sash cord for the neck strap and waist ties. Thread the cords through the eyelets, knotting the ends to keep them in place.

Mood Indigo

The best way to achieve this look is to make the patchwork in denim cut from second-hand clothes,

as this will be more varied in colour, weave and texture than that available at fabric shops.

Second-hand denim has a unique worn and faded quality that you will not get with new cloth.

You will need:

Thirty-six 15 x 18cm (6 x 7¹⁄₄in) pieces of denim fabric in assorted patterns for the apron

240cm (96in) length of 2.5cm (1in) wide cotton tape for neck strap and waist ties

350cm (140in) length of 2.5cm (1in) wide bias binding

Pattern paper

Sewing machine

Needle and matching sewing thread

Take 1.5cm (⁵⁄₈in) seam allowances throughout unless otherwise stated

Note:

Remember to use fabrics of similar weights for patchwork.

1.

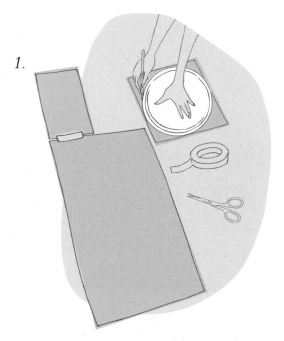

To make the L-shaped apron pattern, cut out a 37.5 x 65cm (15 x 26in) rectangle and a 13 x 30cm (5¹⁄₄ x 12in) rectangle from paper. Place the smaller rectangle with one short edge touching one short edge of the larger rectangle, with one long edge of each aligned, to create an L shape with the longest edge measuring 95cm (38in). Stick together with masking tape. Cut out a 15cm (6in) square of pattern paper and place a round tray 30cm (12in) in diameter over the bottom left-hand corner so the rim touches the two sides. With a pencil, draw around the tray to round off the corner. Carefully cut along the pencil line and insert the cut-off corner into the angle where the large and small rectangles meet. Stick in place with masking tape.

2. Lay the assorted fabric rectangles out on your work surface in six rows of six pieces each and move them around until you have a pleasing arrangement.

3.

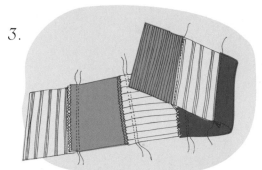

Starting with the first row, pin and machine stitch the longer sides of the rectangles together. Zigzag stitch or pink the seam allowances, press together to one side and topstitch through all the layers to keep the selvedges flat against the wrong side of the fabric. Repeat with the remaining five rows of rectangles. Lay the finished strips on your work surface in the correct order. Pin and machine stitch together, aligning the seams. Zigzag stitch or pink the seam allowances, press together to one side and topstitch through all the layers.

4.

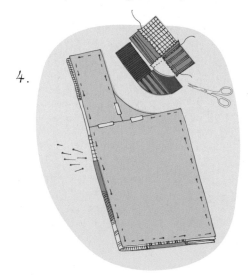

With wrong sides together, fold the patchwork panel in half vertically and lay the L shape apron pattern directly on top, with the longest edge aligned to the fold. Pin the pattern to the fabric and cut out, carefully cutting into the curved angle as the cut-off pieces will be used to make the pouch pocket.

5.

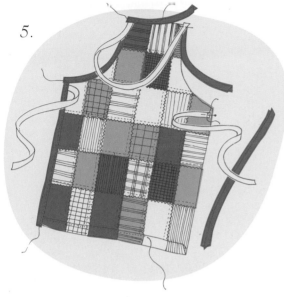

Open out the apron and make a DOUBLE HEM at the bottom edge, following the instructions on page 114 and turning under 1.5cm (⁵/₈in) each time. Cut two 90cm (36in) lengths of cotton tape for the waist ties and attach one to the wrong side of each apron side. Make a DOUBLE HEM at the free end to neaten. Cut two 64cm (25¹/₂in) lengths of bias binding and bind the straight apron sides, covering the edges of the waist ties and neatly finishing the ends at the apron hem. Cut two 52cm (21in) lengths of bias binding, bind the curved apron sides and neatly finish the ends. Cut a 60cm (24in) length of cotton tape for the neck strap and attach each end to the wrong side of the apron bib. Cut a 30cm (12in) length of bias binding and bind the top of the bib, covering the ends of the neck strap and neatly finishing both ends.

6. To make the pouch pocket, machine stitch the two fabric remnants right sides together to make a half circle. Make a 1.5cm (⁵/₈in) DOUBLE HEM along the top edge. Cut an 88cm (35in) length of bias binding, bind the curved pocket edge and neatly finish the ends. Pin the pocket to the apron front, tack and machine stitch in place, as close as possible to the edge of the binding.

Butcher's Boy

This take on the classic butcher's apron has the pint-sized gourmet in mind. For the traditionalist, the style can be made in navy blue cotton twill with a narrow white stripe, or in fresh, tablecloth check for a classic country look. The fabric used here is a neat ticking stripe. The apron features a little patch pocket and practical pouch, plus a neck strap and waist ties in sturdy cotton tape.

You will need:

45cm (18in) length of 112cm (45in) wide ticking stripe cotton fabric for the apron and pockets

130cm (52in) length of 2.5cm (1in) wide woven cotton tape for neck strap and waist ties

138cm (55¼in) length of 2.5cm (1in) wide bias binding

Pattern paper

Sewing machine

Needle and matching sewing thread

Note:

Appliqué or embroider the initials of your little one onto the bib to add that personal touch.

1. To make the apron pattern, draw a rectangle 43 x 23cm (17 x 9¼in) on paper and cut out. Take the longer left side of the rectangle as the centre front of the apron. Draw a line from left to right across the pattern piece, 27cm (10¾in) above the bottom edge. Measure 9cm (3½in) in from the centre front along this line and the same along the top of the rectangle. Draw a line joining these two points. Place a bowl measuring 14.5cm (5¾in) in diameter into the angle formed by the two lines, with the rim touching both lines. Draw around the bowl to round off the corner. Carefully cut away the rectangle with the one curved corner, to be used as the pattern for the pouch pocket.

2.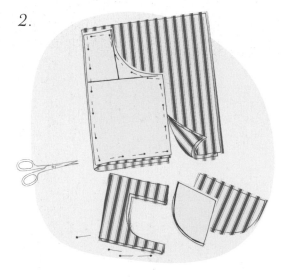

With wrong sides together and aligning the selvedges, fold your chosen fabric in half lengthways. Pin the apron paper pattern to the fabric, ensuring the centre front edge is aligned with the folded edge, and cut out. With the long edge without a curve aligned with the folded edge of the fabric, pin the pouch pocket pattern to the fabric and cut out.

3. Open out the apron and DOUBLE HEM the straight sides, as described on page 114, turning under 1.5cm (5/8in) each time, and inserting one end of a 40cm (16in) length of woven cotton tape into each of the folded edges 1.5cm (5/8in) below the top. DOUBLE HEM the ends of the tapes, turning under 5mm (¼in) each time. DOUBLE HEM bottom edge of apron, turning under 1.5cm (5/8in) each time.

4.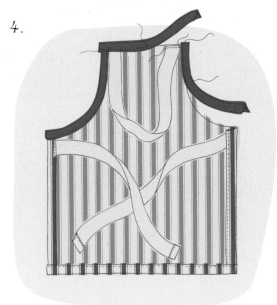

Cut two 26cm (10¼in) lengths of bias binding and bind the curved apron sides, as described in BINDING AN EDGE on page 112. Cut a 50cm (20in) length of cotton tape for the neck strap and attach each end to the wrong side of the apron bib. Cut a 22cm (8¾in) length of bias binding and bind the top of the bib, ensuring the binding covers the ends of the neck strap and is neatly finished at both ends.

5.

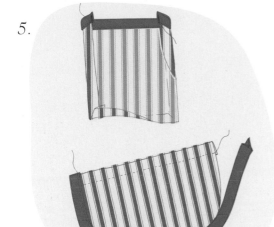

To make the small patch pocket, cut out a 13 x 15cm (5$\frac{1}{4}$ x 6in) rectangle in stripe fabric. Cut a 14cm (5$\frac{1}{2}$in) length of bias binding and bind the top edge. Turn under the pocket sides, pin to the apron and topstitch in place. DOUBLE HEM the long straight edge of the pouch pocket, turning under 1.5cm (5/8in) each time. Cut a 50cm (20in) length of bias binding, bind the pouch edge and neatly finish the ends. Pin the pouch to the apron front, placing it over the small patch pocket, tack and machine stitch in place, as close as possible to the edge of the binding.

Singapore Sling

The minimalist cut of this flared tunic has an oriental 60s swing to it, although the highly theatrical print of floral clusters projected against a garland trellis backdrop is 30s Hollywood in character. Designed to slip over the head and tie at the sides, this stylish and streamlined cover-up will accommodate many body types. An exceedingly tidy style with a lively citrus freshness.

You will need:

100cm (40in) length of 112cm (45in) wide floral print fabric for apron and pocket

520cm (508in) length of 2.5cm (1in) wide bias binding

Sewing machine

Needle and matching sewing threads

Take 1.5cm (⅝in) seam allowances throughout unless otherwise stated

1. Using apron pattern H in the pull-out section and pocket pattern 8 on page 122, pin both patterns to the fabric, making sure that the fabric repeat on the pocket lines up with the same repeat at the bottom of the apron. Cut out one pocket and two apron pieces for front and back panels.

2. Bind the top straight edge of the pocket with a 54cm (21½in) length of bias binding, as described in BINDING AN EDGE on page 112.

3.

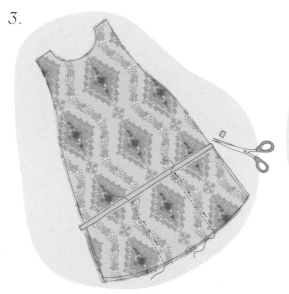

Lay one apron piece on your work surface right side up and place the pocket on top. Aligning the raw edges, pin, tack and machine stitch the pocket to the apron, stitching 5mm (¼in) in from the edges. Measuring the top edge of the pocket, divide it into three equal parts and pin from top to bottom. Machine stitch through the pocket and apron layers along the pinned line to create three pouches, reinforcing the top edges with additional stitching.

4.

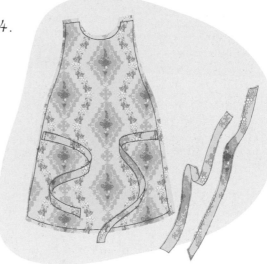

To make the waist ties, cut out four 5 x 40cm (2 x 16in) strips from the remaining fabric. Make a DOUBLE HEM, as described on page 114, on both long sides of one strip, folding over by 5mm (¼in) each time. Pin, tack and stitch in place. Turn over and stitch one short end. Repeat for the other three strips. With wrong sides together, attach a tie to each side of the apron at waist level – approximately 29cm (11½in) above the hemline.

5. With right sides together, sew the apron pieces together across the shoulders. Zigzag stitch or trim the seam allowances with pinking shears to stop the edges fraying.

6.

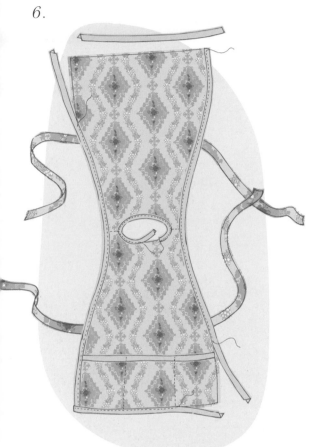

Bind each side of the apron with a 140cm (56in) length of bias binding, ensuring the raw edges of the pocket, waist ties and shoulder seams are all neatly tucked inside the binding. Bind the neckline with a 70cm (28in) length of bias binding, and the front and back apron hems with a 58cm (23in) length of bias binding each, making sure the ends of the bindings are neatly tucked under.

Nimble Fingers (page 92)

Polly Pocket (page 108)

Floral Dance (page 96)

Simple Sampler (page 102)

Pure & Simple (page 100)

Pretty Pastoral (page 104)

Teatime Treat (page 98)

chapter 6

Country Charm

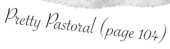

Nimble Fingers

Patience and a very delicate touch are required to give this dainty apron a precious, heirloom look. Choose the colours, patterns and textures for your fabrics and trimmings carefully. This version appears in various tones of fresh lemon and turquoise to create a delightfully summery feel.

You will need:

15cm (6in) length of 90cm (36in) wide stripe fabric for waistband

15cm (6in) length of 112cm (45in) wide plain fabric for upper apron panel

35cm (14in) length of 112cm (45in) wide sprig print fabric for middle panel, frill and pocket

40cm (16in) length of 112cm (45in) wide floral print fabric for lower panel and ties

Selection of satin ribbons in various colours and widths

68cm (27in) length of rickrack

164cm (66in) length of 2cm (⁷/₈in) wide contrast cotton webbing

Sewing machine

Needle and matching sewing threads

Take 1.5cm (⁵/₈in) seam allowances throughout unless otherwise stated

1. To make the upper apron panel, cut out a 13 x 68cm (5¹/₄ x 27in) rectangle in plain fabric. Pin a 68cm (27in) length of rickrack along the whole length of the panel in the centre. Tack and machine stitch to the fabric.

2.

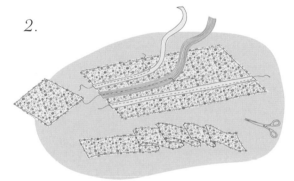

From the sprig print fabric, cut out a 17 x 68cm (7 x 27in) rectangle for the middle panel, an 11 x 100cm (4¹/₂ x 40in) strip for the frill and a 15.5 x 17cm (6¹/₄ x 7in) rectangle for the pocket. Cut out a 19 x 68cm (7¹/₂ x 27in) rectangle for the lower panel in floral print fabric. Pin three 68cm (27in) lengths of ribbon, spaced slightly apart, across the centre of both the middle and the lower panels. Tack and machine stitch to the fabric.

3. Fold a 17cm (7in) length of 2cm (⁷/₈in) wide cotton webbing in half lengthways, gently pressing as you fold, and use to bind one of the 17cm (7in) pocket edges, as described in BINDING AN EDGE on page 112.

4. Make a DOUBLE HEM on both short ends of the frill strip, as described on page 114, folding over 5mm (¹/₄in) and then 1cm (¹/₂in). Pin, tack and machine stitch in place. Fold a 100cm (40in) length of 2cm (⁷/₈in) wide cotton webbing in half lengthways and use to bind one long edge of the fabric strip, as described in BINDING AN EDGE, tucking in any excess webbing at both ends.

5.

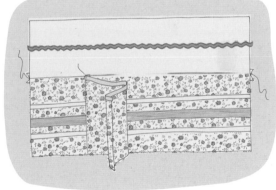

With right sides together, stitch the upper panel to the middle panel along one long edge. Lay out the joined panels flat, right side up, on your work surface. Fold over 1.5cm (⁵/₈in) to the wrong side on both side edges of the pocket and lay it on top of the middle apron panel, matching the top of the bound edge with the seam between the panels. Pin, tack and machine stitch in place.

6. With right sides together, stitch the middle panel
to the lower panel. GATHER the frill strip by hand or
machine, as described in GATHERING – BY HAND or
GATHERING – BY MACHINE on pages 114–115, so that
it measures 62cm (25in). With right sides together,
aligning the raw edges, lay the frill along the edge
of the lower panel, ensuring the frill is 3cm (1¼in)
short of the apron panel at each end. Pin, tack
and machine stitch together. Press both selvedges
towards the side of the lower panel and stitch
through all three fabric layers, as close as possible
to the fold.

7.

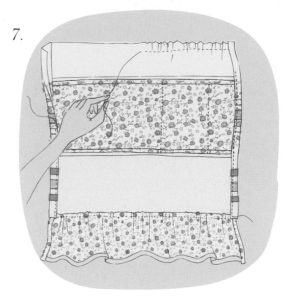

Make a DOUBLE HEM on both sides of the apron,
turning under 1.5cm (⅝in) each time. Pin, tack
and machine stitch in place. GATHER – BY HAND
the top edge of the apron so that it measures
44cm (17½in) across.

8.

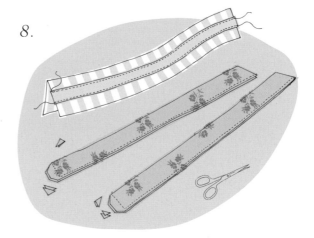

Cut out a 13 x 47cm (5 x 19in) rectangle in stripe
fabric for the waistband. With wrong sides together,
fold in half lengthways and press in a crease. Open
out the waistband and pin a 47cm (19in) length of
2cm (⅞in) wide cotton webbing along the centre
of one side. Tack and stitch in place. Cut out two
8 x 48cm (3¼ x 19in) strips in floral print fabric for
the waist ties. To make the waistband, follow steps
2–4 in WAISTBAND – WITH WAIST TIES on page 119.

Floral Dance

These finely drawn spring flowers literally gambol across this charming half apron in a fever of

excitement, their exuberant hues reverberating out into the vivid trims. Wear this pinnie and

no one will be left in doubt that spring has sprung! The colour palette may be bold and brilliant

but the mood is gentle and ultra-feminine, suggested by the softly gathered waist and pocket.

You will need:

55cm (22in) length of 112cm (45in) wide floral print fabric for apron panel and pocket

30cm (12in) length of 112cm (45in) wide plain fabric for waistband and ties

25cm (10in) length of 112cm (45in) wide plain contrast fabric for frill

8 x 20cm (3¹/₄ x 8in) piece of plain contrast fabric for pocket binding

Sewing machine

Needle and matching sewing threads

Take 1.5cm (⁵/₈in) seam allowances throughout unless otherwise stated

1. Using apron pattern E in the pull-out section and pocket pattern 2 on page 121, pin both patterns to the floral print fabric. Cut out one apron piece and two pocket pieces.

2. Cut out three 7.5 x 103cm (3 x 41in) strips of plain fabric for the frill. Machine stitch together to make one long piece. Zigzag stitch or trim the seam allowances with pinking shears to stop the edges fraying. Make a DOUBLE HEM along one long length of the fabric strip, as described on page 114, folding over 5mm (¹/₄in) each time.

3. GATHER the frill by hand or machine along the other long raw edge to 147cm (58in), as described on pages 114–115. With right sides together, aligning the raw edges, lay the frill along the curved edge of the apron skirt. Pin, tack and machine stitch in place. Zigzag stitch or trim the seam allowances with pinking shears to stop the edges fraying.

5.

Cut out a 5 x 17.5cm (2 x 7in) strip of plain contrast fabric, press in half lengthways and, with right sides together, attach one side of the strip to the top of the pocket, taking a 1cm (³/₈in) seam allowance. Fold the strip over to the rear of the pocket, fold under 1cm (³/₈in) and attach with slipstitch, ensuring any excess binding is neatly tucked out of view. Sink machine stitches through both the pocket and apron layers. Reinforce the ends with additional stitches.

4.

Place the two pocket pieces right sides together and machine stitch along the curved edges from one end to the other, taking a 1cm (³/₈in) seam allowance. Snip into the seam allowance and turn right side out. With raw edges together, GATHER the top of the pocket to 15.5cm (6¹/₄in).

6.

GATHER the top of the apron in the centre, so the total measurement across the top (including frill) is 45cm (18in). Cut out a 15 x 49cm (6 x 19¹/₂in) rectangle for the waistband and two 9 x 48cm (3¹/₂ x 19in) strips for the waist ties in plain contrast fabric. Follow the instructions for the WAISTBAND – WITH WAIST TIES, as described on page 119.

Teatime Treat

Nothing evokes the high teas of a bygone era more vividly than a dainty, freshly laundered tablecloth, the floral patterns of 'Sunday Best' crockery mimicking the embroidered motifs scattered on the tabletop. This quaint and feminine apron, with its hand-stitched, hand-me-down appearance is the ideal choice to wear on such occasions, bringing with it a sense of wellbeing and contentment. Fresh gingham ribbon and broderie anglaise trim add colour and texture, and make this the perfect style for spring.

You will need:

Vintage embroidered tablecloth for apron

15cm (6in) length of 112cm (45in) wide plain fabric for waistband

10cm (4in) length of 112cm (45in) wide gingham check fabric for waist ties

80cm (32in) length of 4cm (1¹/₂in) wide broderie anglaise/eyelet trim

6 x 80cm (32in) lengths of 1.5cm (⁵/₈in) wide gingham ribbons in various colours

48cm (19in) length of 1.5cm (⁵/₈in) wide satin ribbon

Sewing machine

Needle and matching sewing threads

Take 1.5cm (⁵/₈in) seam allowances throughout unless otherwise stated

1. To make the apron panel, cut out a 51 x 78cm (20 x 31in) rectangle from an embroidered tablecloth, ensuring the floral motifs are in a central position. With right sides together, align the raw edge of the apron hem with the eyelet trim and stitch together. Steam-press the selvedge towards the apron side, and sink machine stitches through all the layers, as close as possible to the seam between the apron and the eyelet edging.

2.

Pin four 80cm (32in) lengths of ribbon, spaced slightly apart, across the bottom of the apron panel, just above the eyelet edging. Tack and machine stitch to the panel. Pin two more 80cm (32in) lengths of ribbon midway across the apron front. Stitch in place. Make a DOUBLE HEM along both short edges of the apron, as described on page 114, folding over by 1.5cm (⁵/₈in) each time.

3.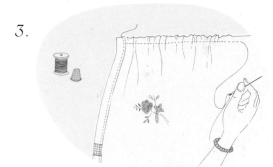

GATHER the apron by hand or machine to 44cm (17¹/₂in) along the top raw edge, as described on pages 114–115.

4.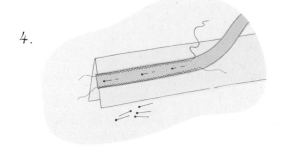

To make the waistband, cut out a 13 x 47cm (5¹/₄ x 18¹/₂in) rectangle in plain fabric. With wrong sides together, fold in half lengthways and press in a crease. Open out the waistband and pin a 48cm (19in) length of satin ribbon along the centre of one side. Tack and stitch in place. Cut out two 8 x 48cm (3¹/₄ x 19in) strips in gingham check fabric for the waist ties. To make the waistband, follow the instructions for WAISTBAND – WITH WAIST TIES on page 119.

Pure & Simple

Taking on Quaker principles, this apron is an ode to restraint. Although its construction is a little fiddly and time-consuming, the end result is sheer simplicity. A regard for symmetry and order is evident in the double row of neat little pockets, clearly defined with narrow bindings to echo the apron's waistband and edges. Gentle colours and rustic fabric textures underscore the sense of purity. This discreet, 'honest-to-goodness' style has timeless appeal. Made well, it will last a lifetime, and your children will end up treasuring it as much as you do.

You will need:

50cm (20in) length of 110cm (44in) wide linen fabric for apron, pockets and waist ties

300cm (120in) length of 2.5cm (1in) wide bias binding in contrast colour

Cotton embroidery thread in contrasting colour

Sewing machine

Needle and matching sewing threads

Tailor's chalk

Take 1.5cm (⅝in) seam allowances throughout unless otherwise stated

1. To make the apron panel, cut out a 44 x 58.5cm (17½ x 23½in) rectangle in linen fabric. Lay the fabric piece right side up on your work surface with the longer edges on each side and the shorter edges at the top and bottom. Round off the bottom corner on each side using tailor's chalk and the curved edge of a round bowl measuring 14.5cm (5¾in) in diameter. Remove the corners by cutting along the chalk line.

2.

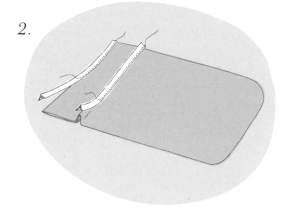

To make the mock waistband, fold over 5cm (2in) along the top of the apron panel to the wrong side and steam-press. Fold another 5cm (2in) and press. Cut a 48cm (19in) length of bias binding and use it to bind the upper folded edge, as described in BINDING AN EDGE on page 112, catching the raw edge that is tucked inside the fold. Open out the pleat and press flat, with the binding pointing downwards. With the apron right side up, bind the other folded edge with a 48cm (19in) length of binding.

3.

Using pocket pattern 5 on page 126, pin the pattern to the linen fabric and cut out four pockets. Bind the top edge of each pocket piece with a 14cm (5½in) length of binding. Fold over 1.5cm (⅝in) to the wrong side on the three remaining sides of each pocket, pleating excess fabric around the bottom corners to round them off neatly. Steam-press flat. Position the four pockets on top of the apron, pin, tack and machine stitch as close as possible to the pocket edges. Add a second row of topstitching to the pockets, 1cm (⅜in) in from the edge, and use this as a guide to hand stitch decorative running stitches in contrasting embroidery thread.

4.

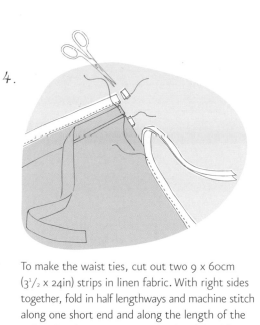

To make the waist ties, cut out two 9 x 60cm (3$\frac{1}{2}$ x 24in) strips in linen fabric. With right sides together, fold in half lengthways and machine stitch along one short end and along the length of the strip. Trim the corners, turn the ties right side out and press. Aligning the raw ends of the ties with the raw edges on each side of the wrong side of the apron, machine stitch to the apron 5mm ($\frac{1}{4}$in) in from the edge.

5. Bind the raw edges of the apron with a 145cm (58in) length of bias binding. Ensure the ends are neatly tucked under at the waist.

Simple Sampler

Antique samplers inspire this basic apron, made special with hand-stitched embellishment at the hem and pocket. Whether embroidering a simple pattern or embarking on a more complicated design such as an alphabet, a namesake or a floral motif, using the checks of the gingham fabric as a sewing guide will ensure your cross stitches are neat and perfectly spaced. If you're short of time, use fabric markers to draw in the crosses. Other embroidered trims such as daisy chains offer a pretty alternative to the rickrack.

You will need:

70cm (28in) length of 112cm (45in) wide gingham fabric for apron panel, all-in-one waistband/ties and pocket

228cm (91in) length of jumbo rickrack in contrast colour

Cotton embroidery threads in contrasting colours

Sewing machine

Needle and matching sewing threads

Take 1.5cm ($^5/_8$in) seam allowances throughout unless otherwise stated

1. Cut out a 50 x 58cm (20 x 23in) rectangle for the apron, two 9 x 83cm ($3^1/_2$ x 33in) strips for the all-in-one waistband and a 17 x 24cm ($6^3/_4$ x $9^1/_2$in) rectangle for the pocket, all in gingham check fabric.

2. Make a DOUBLE HEM, as described on page 114, turning under by 1.5cm ($^5/_8$in) each time to the wrong side along both short edges and one long edge of the apron panel. Cut a 52cm (21in) length of rickrack and stitch it across the apron front, 8cm ($3^1/_4$in) above the hemline, turning under the ends for a neat finish. Cut a 142cm (57in) length of rickrack and machine stitch it along the hem and down the sides of the apron front.

3.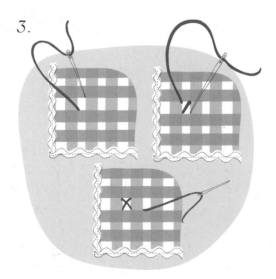

Sew cross stitches with contrast embroidery threads inside the rectangle created by the lines of rickrack across the bottom of the apron.

4.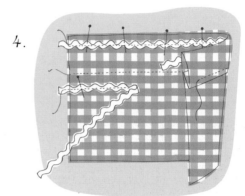

For the pocket, make a DOUBLE HEM along one short edge, folding over by 1.5cm ($^5/_8$in) and then by 5cm (2in). Machine stitch two 17cm ($6^3/_4$in) lengths of rickrack onto the pocket and sew cross stitches between them. Fold the remaining three sides of the pocket over by 1.5cm ($^5/_8$in) to the wrong side. Lay the pocket on the apron front, pin and machine stitch in place.

5.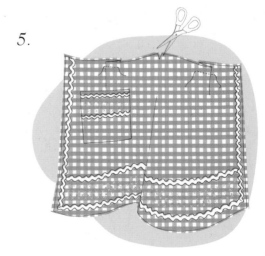

Make two 2cm ($^7/_8$in) pleats in the top raw edge of the apron, reducing the width to 44cm ($17^1/_2$in), and machine stitch the pleats in place. As a guide, fold the apron in half lengthways and mark the centre front by cutting a small notch in the fabric at the top edge.

6. To make the waistband, follow the instructions as described in Waistband – Two-Piece/All-In-One on page 118.

Pretty Pastoral

The ill-fated Queen of France, Marie Antoinette, would have fallen in love with this pinnie. In fact, she probably would have lost her head over it! This would have been the perfect choice of attire for leading her lambs through the fields surrounding the Hameau, her 'play farm', at Versailles. Made from toile de Jouy and trimmed with lace, this frothy confection has the bucolic charm of a Fragonard painting.

You will need:

60cm (24in) length of 280cm (112in) wide toile de Jouy fabric for the apron, flounces, neck and waist ties

360cm (144in) length of 3.5cm (1³/₈in) wide lace trim

Pattern paper

Sewing machine

Needle and matching sewing threads

Take 1.5cm (⁵/₈in) seam allowances throughout unless otherwise stated

1.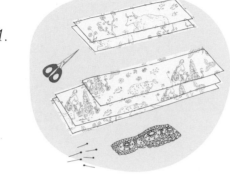

Cut out a 14 x 66cm (5¹/₂ x 26¹/₄in) and a 19 x 66cm (7¹/₂ x 26¹/₄in) rectangle for the underskirt, a 16 x 87cm (6¹/₄ x 34³/₄in) strip for the top flounce and two 21 x 123cm (8¹/₄ x 49in) strips for the middle and bottom flounces, all in toile de Jouy.

2. Make a DOUBLE HEM on both ends and one long side of all three flounces, as described on page 114, turning under by 9mm (³/₈in) and then by 5mm (¹/₄in). Pin, tack and machine stitch the hems as close as possible to the folded edges.

3.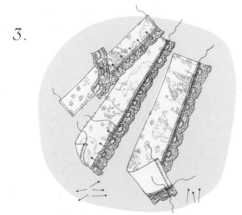

Cut one 88cm (35¹/₄in) length of lace trim and attach to the long hemmed edge of the top flounce, and cut two 124cm (49¹/₂in) lengths of lace trim and attach to the long hemmed edge of the middle and bottom flounces. Machine stitch in place, using a small zigzag stitch, and neatly fold the ends of the lace trim under the flounces to finish.

4.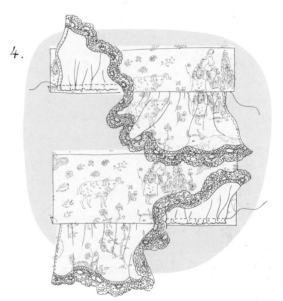

GATHER the middle and bottom flounces to a length of 60cm (24in), as described in GATHERING — BY HAND on page 114 or GATHERING — BY MACHINE on page 115. Attach the gathered edge of the bottom flounce to the bottom edge of the apron's larger underskirt panel, ensuring the flounce is 3cm (1¹/₄in) short of the panel at each end. Attach the gathered edge of the middle flounce to the bottom edge of the apron's smaller underskirt panel, ensuring the flounce is 3cm (1¹/₄in) short of the panel at each end.

5. With right sides together and aligning the raw edges, attach the upper and lower panels of the underskirt. DOUBLE HEM the apron sides, turning under by 1.5cm (⁵/₈in) each time.

6.

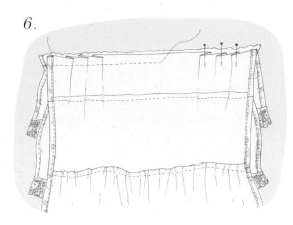

Reduce the top waist of the underskirt to 42cm (16³/₄in) by making three 1.5cm (⁵/₈in) deep pleats at each side. GATHER the top flounce to 42cm (16³/₄in), pin it to the waist of the underskirt, align the raw edges and sew together.

7. To make the tapered bib pattern, draw a 25cm (10in) square onto pattern paper and cut out. Taking one of the sides as the top edge of the bib, measure in 2.5cm (1in) at both ends. From each of these points, draw a line down to their corresponding corners at the bottom left- and right-hand corners. Cut along each line to taper the pattern piece.

8. To make the apron bib, pin the paper pattern to the fabric and cut out. Cut out one 4.5 x 22cm (1³/₄ x 8³/₄in) and two 4.5 x 70cm (1³/₄ x 28in) strips of fabric, and follow the instructions in BINDING AN EDGE on page 112.

9.

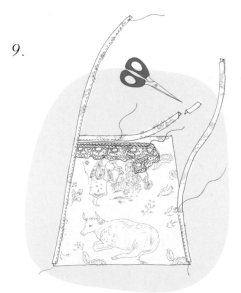

BIND the top edge of the bib with the short binding, trimming the ends so they follow the line of the bib sides. Cut a 20cm (8in) length of lace trim and sew it to the bib, below the attached binding. Bind each side of the bib with a 70cm (28in) strip of bindings. Pin and tack along the whole length of the bindings and close with machine stitches, overlapping the ends to finish.

10.

Fold the apron and bib in half lengthways, and snip into the edge of the fabric to mark the centre front points. Align the raw edges, match up the centre front notches and lay the reverse side of the bib onto the wrong side of the apron. Pin, tack and machine stitch together, 1.5cm ($^5/_8$in) in from the edge.

11. To make the 'all-in-one' waistband/waist ties, cut out a 9 x 153cm ($3^1/_2$ x $61^1/_4$in) strip of printed cotton fabric and follow instructions for WAISTBAND – TWO PIECE/ALL-IN-ONE, as described on page 118.

12. Press the waistband towards the bib and secure with a row of topstitching through all the fabric layers.

Polly Pocket

Taking its cue from the cheerleader, this playful 'rah-rah skirt' style is fun and flirty, fresh and modern. Made from two half circles in contrasting fabric, sewn together and turned right side out, the apron offers the option of a plain or patterned look. The pockets are faced with a layer of plain fabric to give attractive contrast. This also gives more substance when attaching the bindings, which introduce splashes of bright colour to give essential bite to the soft and delicate print. For a true take on retro style, omit the pockets and replace with a poodle appliqué, adding multiple rows of rickrack braid to both hemline and waistband.

You will need:

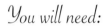

70cm (28in) length of 112cm (45in) wide floral print fabric for outer apron panel and pockets

90cm (36in) length of 112cm (45in) wide plain fabric for inner apron panel, pockets, waistband and waist ties

56cm (22¼in) lengths of 2cm (⅞in) wide bias binding in each of two complementary colours

Pattern Paper

Sewing machine

Needle and matching sewing threads

Take 1.5cm (⅝in) seam allowances throughout unless otherwise stated

1.

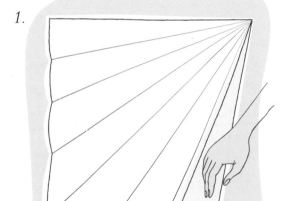

Cut out a 58cm (22¾in) paper square. Fold the square in half diagonally. Fold the two halves created in half again. Repeat the process until you have a folded fan effect comprising eight equal segments.

2.

Open out the paper square. From the top right-hand corner (where all the folds begin) and along every fold line, measure 14cm (5½in) and mark all points with a pen. From these points, measure out 41cm (16¼in) and, again, mark all points. Join together both series of dots to create a small and a large curve. Cutting carefully along the curves, remove the top right and bottom left corners to create a semicircular skirt pattern.

3.

Fold the floral print fabric in half lengthways, lay the paper pattern on top with one of the straight sides lining up with the centre fold and pin together. Cut around the paper pattern. Repeat this step with the plain fabric.

4.

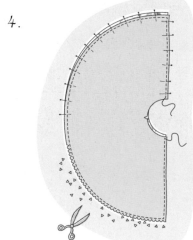

Open out both fabric pieces and, with right sides facing and all edges aligned, pin, tack and machine stitch together the two straight sides and the larger curved edge. Cut off the sharp corners, trim down the seam allowances, and cut out wedge shapes along the curved edge.

5. Turn the half circle skirt right side out and steam-press the edges before topstitching 5mm ($^1/_4$in) in from the edge.

6.

Secure the smaller curve 12mm ($^1/_2$in) in from the edge with machine stitches. Snip into the seam allowance to straighten the curve in readiness for attaching the waistband.

7. To make the patch pockets, cut out two circles in floral print fabric and two in plain fabric, using a 16cm ($6^1/_4$in) diameter plate as a template. With wrong sides together, place a floral print circle over a plain one and stitch together 5mm ($^1/_4$in) in from the edge. Cut a 54cm ($21^1/_2$in) length of binding and attach to the edge of the circle following the steps described in BINDING AN EDGE on page 112. Repeat with the remaining pocket, using the contrast colour bias binding.

8. Pin the first pocket to the apron and topstitch over the existing stitching, approximately three quarters of the way around the binding, leaving sufficient space for the hand at the top. Overlap beneath with the second pocket, repeating the stitching method. Fold down the top section of each pocket and press in place.

9. Cut out a 12 x 48cm ($4^3/_4$ x $18^3/_4$in) strip of plain fabric for the waistband and follow the steps in WAISTBAND – BASIC on page 117.

10. To make the waist ties, cut out two 8 x 70cm ($3^1/_4$ x 28in) strips of plain fabric and follow the steps described in WAIST TIES – QUICK 'N' EASY on page 119. Pin a tie to one side of the inner waistband. Stitch vertically in place, trim the selvedge, fold the waist tie back on itself and machine stitch again, making sure the trimmed selvedge is no longer visible. Repeat with the remaining waist tie.

Basic techniques

APPLIQUÉ

1. Create a template by transferring the design motif onto thin card. Cut out.

2. Cut a square of paper-backed, iron-on double-sided appliqué adhesive large enough to accommodate the design motif. Lay the square, adhesive side down, onto the wrong side of an equal-sized fabric square to be used for the appliqué and press with a hot iron to heat bond.

3. Place the template onto the paper-backed side of the fabric and draw around with a pencil.

4. Carefully cut out the motif and peel away the paper backing.

5. Place the motif, adhesive side down, onto the fabric base in the desired position and press with a hot iron to attach.

6. For a professional finish, machine stitch all the way around the motif with a small zigzag stitch.

BINDING AN EDGE

 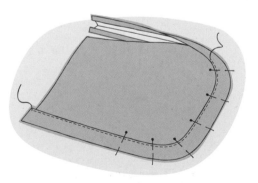

1. Fold a length of bias binding over lengthways, gently steam-pressing as you fold.

2. Neatly insert the raw edge of the fabric to be bound into the folded binding. Pin, tack and machine stitch in place. NOTE: Ease the binding around corners with a steam iron before sewing to avoid puckering.

BOWS – CRISSCROSS

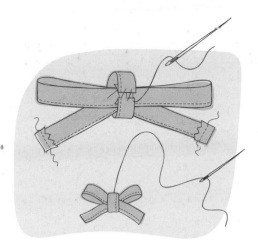

1. Fold over lengthways a strip of bias binding. Pin, tack and machine stitch. Form the strip into a crisscross loop and secure with a few stitches.

2. Wrap a small strip of bias binding around the middle of the loop, securing with a few stitches at the back.

BOWS – TAILORED

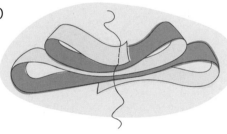

1. Cut a length of satin ribbon and zigzag into a double-layered loop. Stitch through all the layers to secure.

2. Cut a smaller length of ribbon and wrap it around the middle of the loop to form a tailored bow, securing it with a few stitches at the back.

CENTRE LINE NOTCH

If the apron patterns are symmetrical, once the fabric pieces have been cut out, fold them in half lengthways and make tiny snips (balance marks) into the seam allowances at top and bottom. When joining pattern pieces together, match up the balance marks to achieve greater accuracy.

DOUBLE HEM

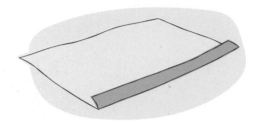

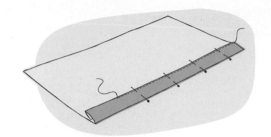

1. Depending on the measurements specified in each project, fold the edge of the fabric over to the wrong side and press.

2. Fold over again, pin, tack, press and machine stitch in place, stitching as close as possible to the folded edge.

FINISHING RAW EDGES

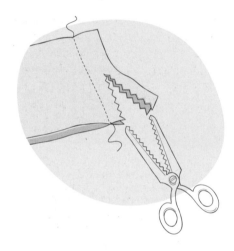

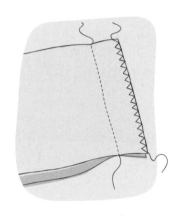

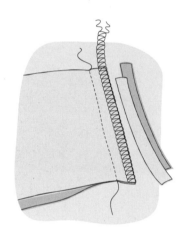

1. Trim the seam allowance with pinking shears.

2. Use the zigzag stitch on your sewing machine with the maximum stitch width and length.

3. For a truly professional finish, use an overlocking machine, which simultaneously trims and over-edge stitches the seam allowance.

GATHERING – BY HAND

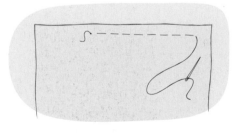

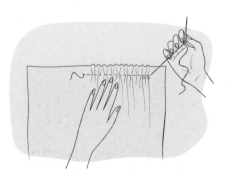

1. Take a needle and thread, and work running stitches along the edge to be gathered.

2. Gently pull the thread to gather the fabric to the required length, making sure the gathers are even. Secure with a few stitches at the end.

GATHERING — BY MACHINE

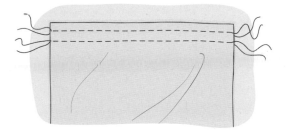

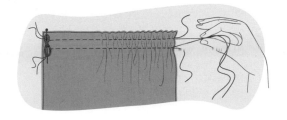

1. Using the longest stitch length, machine stitch two parallel lines 1cm (½in) apart along the edge to be gathered.

2. Secure all the threads at one end with a pin and gently pull the two top threads at the other end to gather the fabric to the required length, making sure the gathers are even. Secure these threads with another pin.

3. When attaching the gathered fabric to another fabric piece, use a normal stitch length and machine stitch between the parallel lines of stitching to secure. Remove the parallel lines of stitching to finish.

PATCH POCKETS — BAGGED-OUT

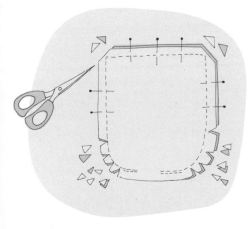

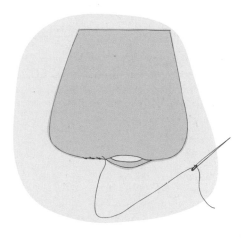

1. Cut out two pockets instead of one. With right sides together and aligning the raw edges, pin and tack the two pocket pieces together. Taking the specified seam allowance, stitch all the way around, leaving a gap at the bottom, wide enough to pull the pocket through, right side out. Trim off right-angled corners, the seam allowance and cut out little wedges around the rounded corners.

2. 'Bag-out' the pocket and carefully press the seamed edges.

3. Tuck inside the exposed seam allowance and neatly slipstitch the opening closed.

PATCH POCKETS – CONTOUR STITCHED

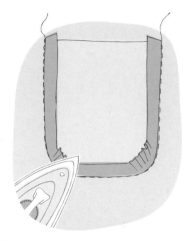

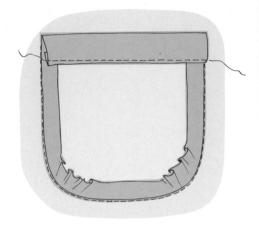

1. Using colour-matched thread, topstitch around the pocket piece along the seam allowance line.

2. Fold over (onto the wrong side) the allowance on the stitched line. Neatly pleat and steam-press the excess fabric as you turn the rounded corner.

3. Double hem the top edge and stitch in place.

PATCH POCKETS – USING A TEMPLATE

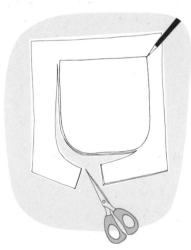

1. Trace the pocket pattern onto thin card and cut out.

2. Cut away the specified seam allowance to make a template of the pocket.

3. Place the template in the centre and onto the wrong side of the fabric piece, and wrap the seam allowance over it, steam-pressing flat as you go around the pocket. Remove the template before attaching the pocket.

SNIPPING CORNERS

Snip diagonally across the seam allowance at the corners to eliminate bulk and to achieve neat right angles when the item is turned right side out.

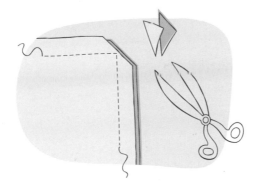
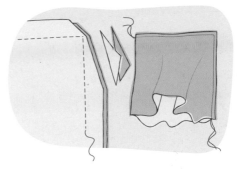

WAISTBAND – BASIC

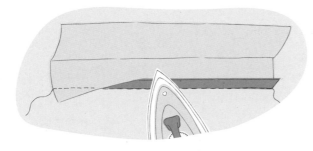

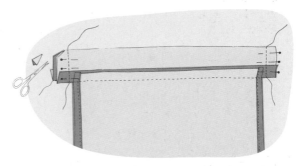

1. To make a basic waistband, cut out a strip of fabric to the size specified in the project. With wrong sides together, fold in half lengthways and lightly press into a crease, to mark the top of the waistband.

2. Machine stitch along the whole length of one edge of the waistband 1.5cm (5/8in) in from the raw edge. This will act as a fold-over guide when you are finishing the inside waistband.

4. Open out the folded waistband and fold back on itself, so that the right sides face each other. Aligning the raw edges of the waistband ends, pin and machine stitch together. Snip the seam allowance diagonally at the corners.

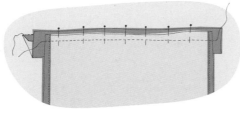

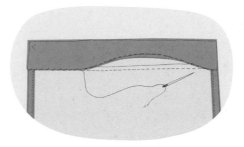

3. Aligning the raw edges, pin the unstitched right side of the waistband to the right side of the apron. Machine stitch together.

5. Turn the waistband right side out and turn under the raw edge of the inside waistband, using the line of machine stitches as a guide. Pin and slipstitch the opening closed.

WAISTBAND — TWO-PIECE/ALL-IN-ONE

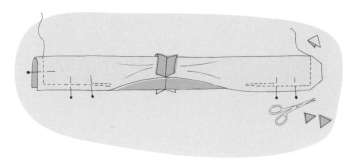

1. To make a two-piece/all-in-one waistband with waist ties, cut out two strips of fabric to the size specified in the project. Machine stitch together to make one long strip. Press open the seam. Fold over lengthways the waistband with right sides together and raw edges aligned. Pin, tack and machine stitch down each of the short ends and along the length of the waistband, leaving a central gap of at least 50cm (20in). Snip each of the four corners, close to the stitching line.

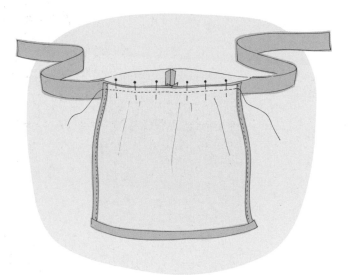

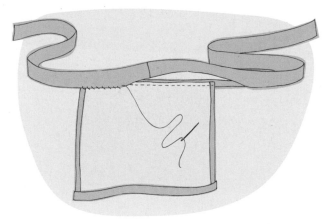

2. Turn the waistband right side out and press. Pin and tack the right side of the apron to one of the open-ended right sides of the waistband, aligning the raw edges and ensuring the centre of the apron matches up with the centre seam of the waistband. Machine stitch in place.

3. Tuck the raw edge of the apron into the gap, along with the unstitched section of the waistband's seam allowance. Close the opening with slipstitches.

WAISTBAND – WITH WAIST TIES

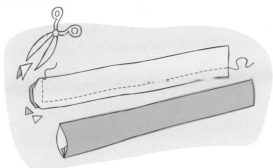

1. To make the waistband, follow steps 1, 2 and 3 in WAISTBAND – BASIC on page 117.

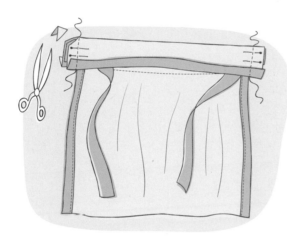

2. To make the waist ties, cut out two strips of fabric to the size specified in the project. With right sides together, fold in half lengthways and machine stitch both strips along one short end and along the length of the strips. Trim the corners and turn the ties right side out.

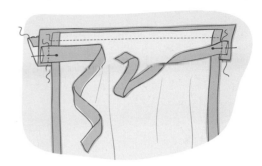

3. Align the raw ends of the waist ties with the ends of the front side of the waistband, ensuring the top edge of the ties lies just below the crease. Pin, tack and machine stitch in place.

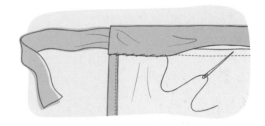

4. Continue with WAISTBAND – BASIC steps 4 and 5 on page 117.

WAIST TIES – QUICK 'N' EASY

1. To make a waist tie, cut out a strip of fabric to the size specified in the project. With right sides together, fold in half lengthways, sandwiching between the layers a length of cotton tape that is longer than the waist tie.

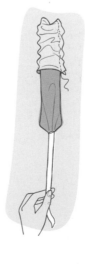

2. Machine stitch the strip along one short end and along the length of the strip.

3. Pull the cotton tape and turn the strip right side out.

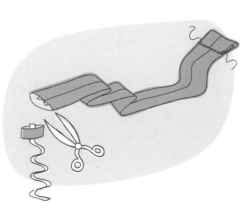

4. Cut off the closed end of the waist tie.

5. Roll the waist tie with your fingers until the seam is located in the centre. Steam-press flat and fold over double one end, securing with machine stitches to finish.

Pocket patterns & appliqué templates

These diagrams are full-size and where applicable, include seam allowances. (The exact amount of seam allowance required is specified in each project as measurements may vary.)

Most diagrams are shown as halves, so the (broken) CENTRE FOLD LINE indicated on the pattern/template must be aligned with the fold of a double layer of fabric before cutting out. Alternatively, a complete pattern/template can be obtained by tracing off the diagram onto a folded piece of pattern paper (remembering to match up the CENTRE FOLD LINE with the fold of the paper) and then opening it out in readiness for pinning to your chosen fabric.

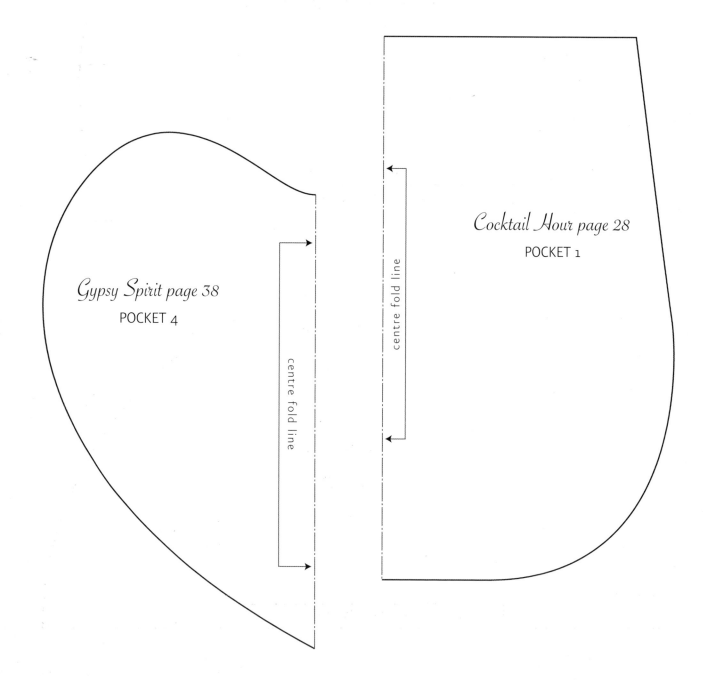

Gypsy Spirit page 38

POCKET 4

centre fold line

Cocktail Hour page 28

POCKET 1

centre fold line

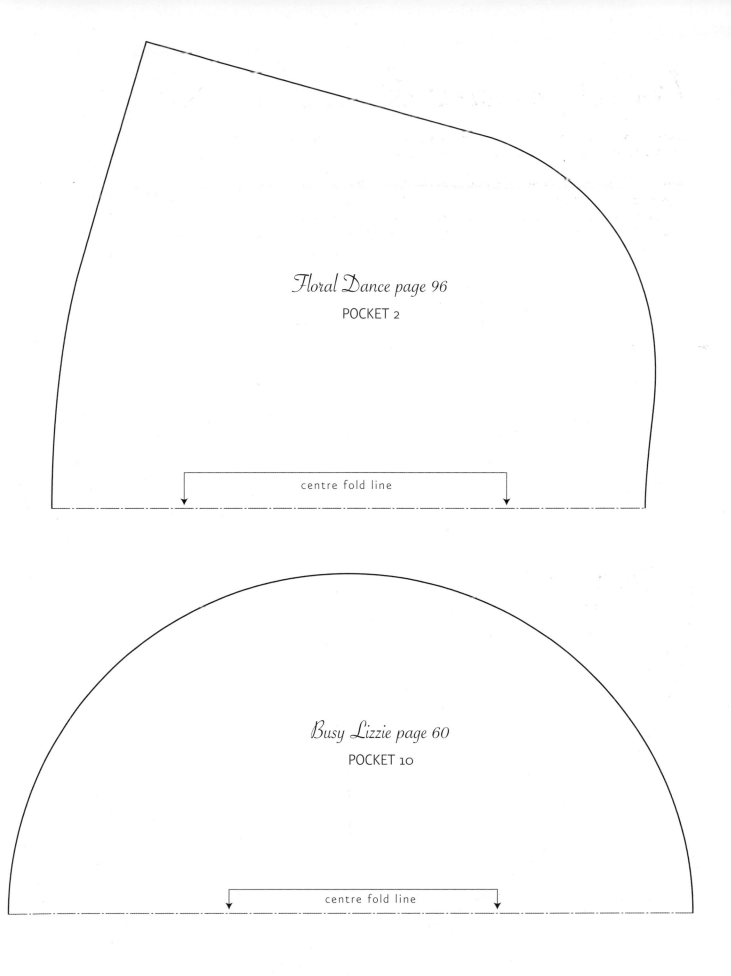

Floral Dance page 96

POCKET 2

centre fold line

Busy Lizzie page 60

POCKET 10

centre fold line

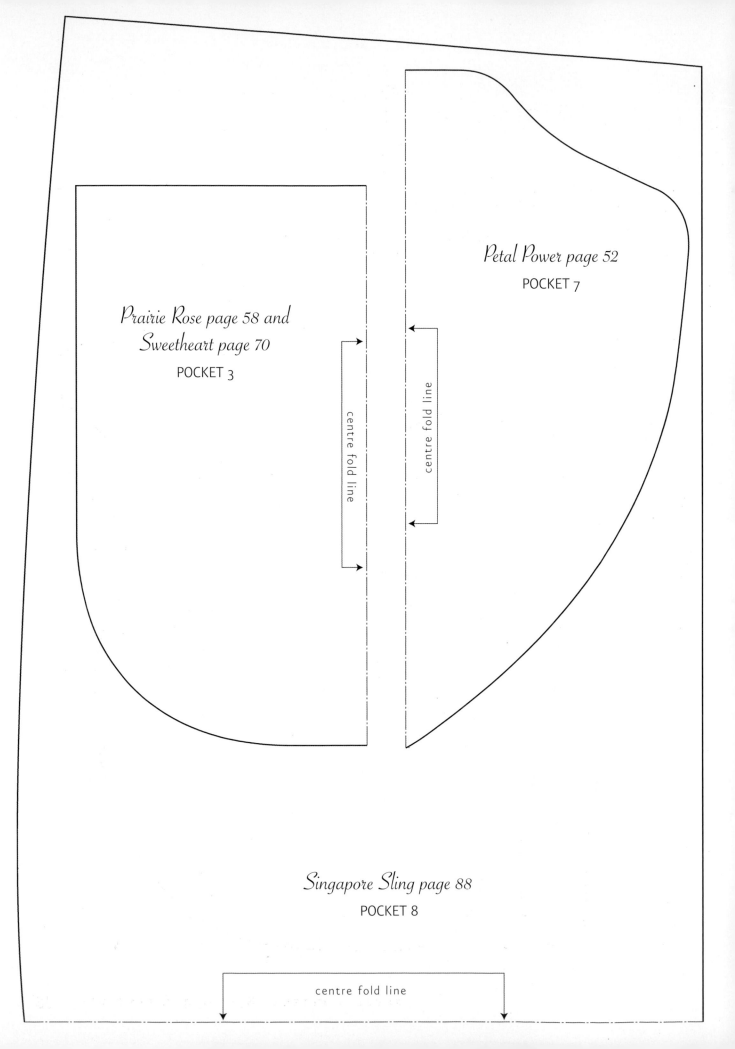

Prairie Rose page 58 and
Sweetheart page 70

POCKET 3

Petal Power page 52

POCKET 7

centre fold line

centre fold line

Singapore Sling page 88

POCKET 8

centre fold line

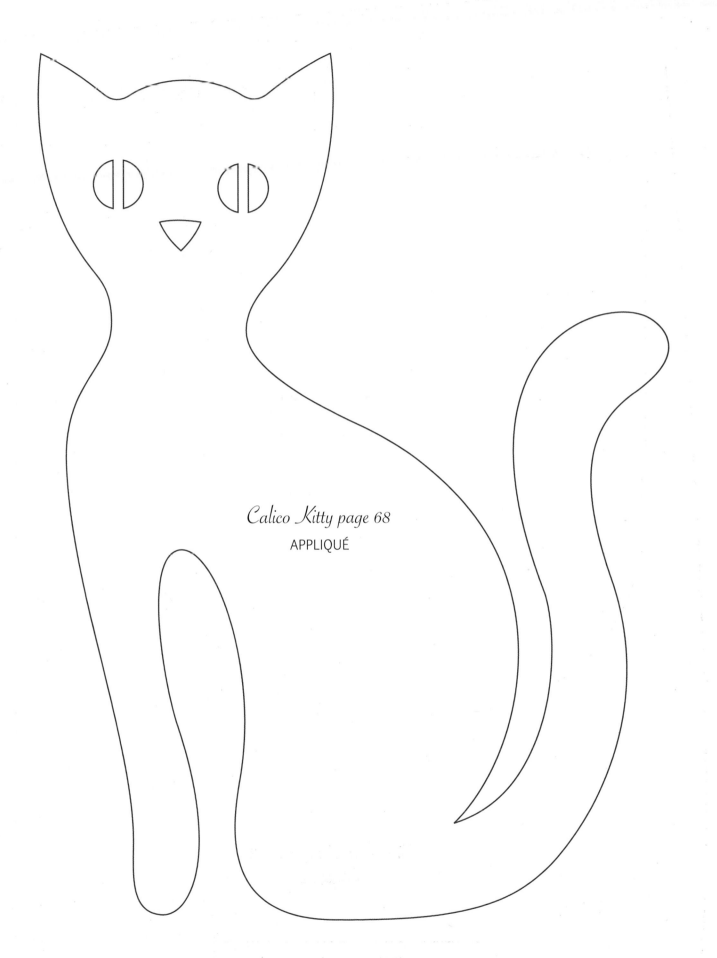

Calico Kitty page 68
APPLIQUÉ

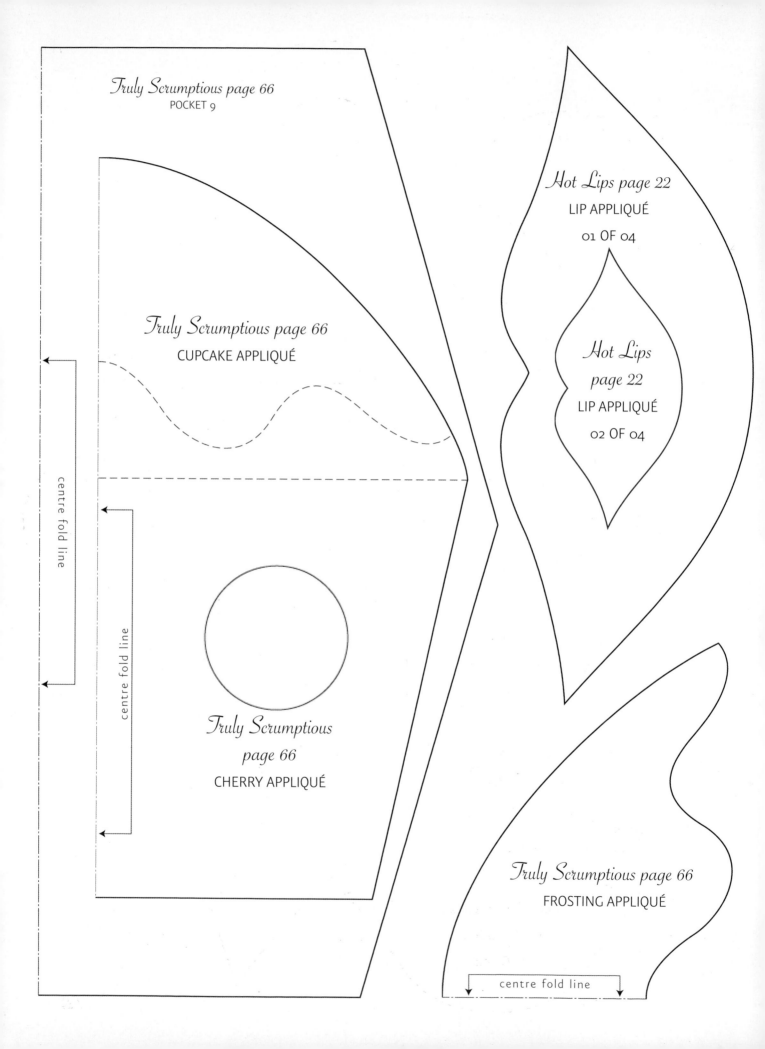

Truly Scrumptious page 66
POCKET 9

Truly Scrumptious page 66
CUPCAKE APPLIQUÉ

centre fold line

centre fold line

Truly Scrumptious
page 66
CHERRY APPLIQUÉ

Hot Lips page 22
LIP APPLIQUÉ
01 OF 04

Hot Lips
page 22
LIP APPLIQUÉ
02 OF 04

Truly Scrumptious page 66
FROSTING APPLIQUÉ

centre fold line

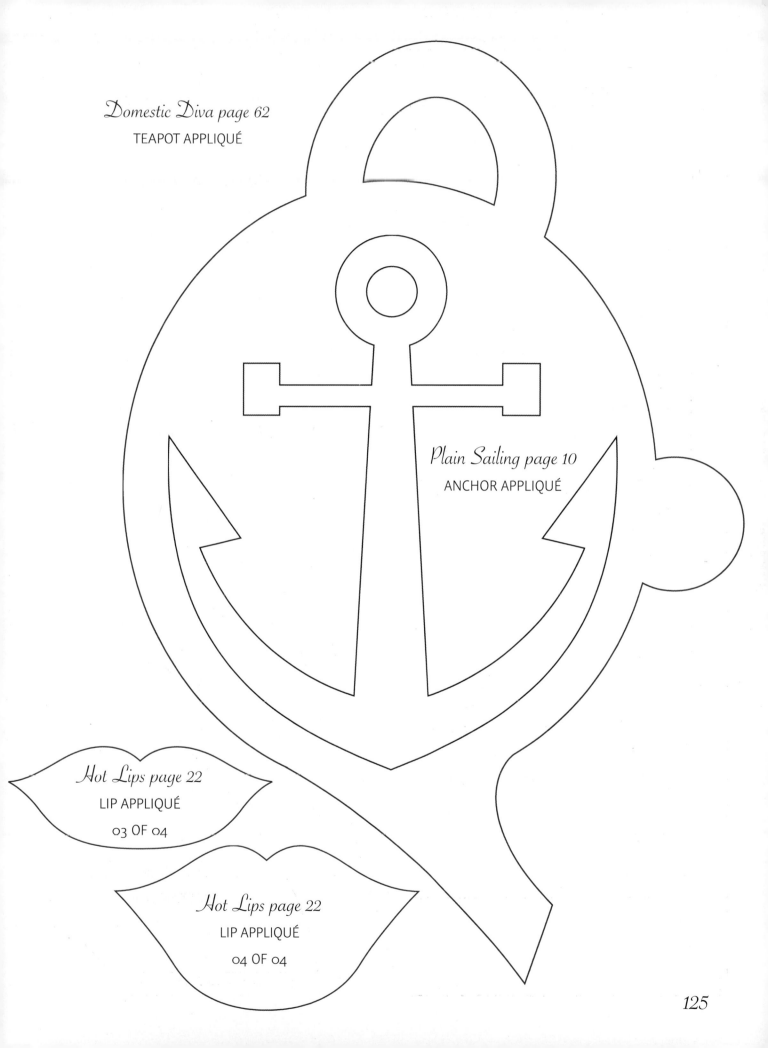

Domestic Diva page 62

TEAPOT APPLIQUÉ

Plain Sailing page 10

ANCHOR APPLIQUÉ

Hot Lips page 22

LIP APPLIQUÉ

03 OF 04

Hot Lips page 22

LIP APPLIQUÉ

04 OF 04

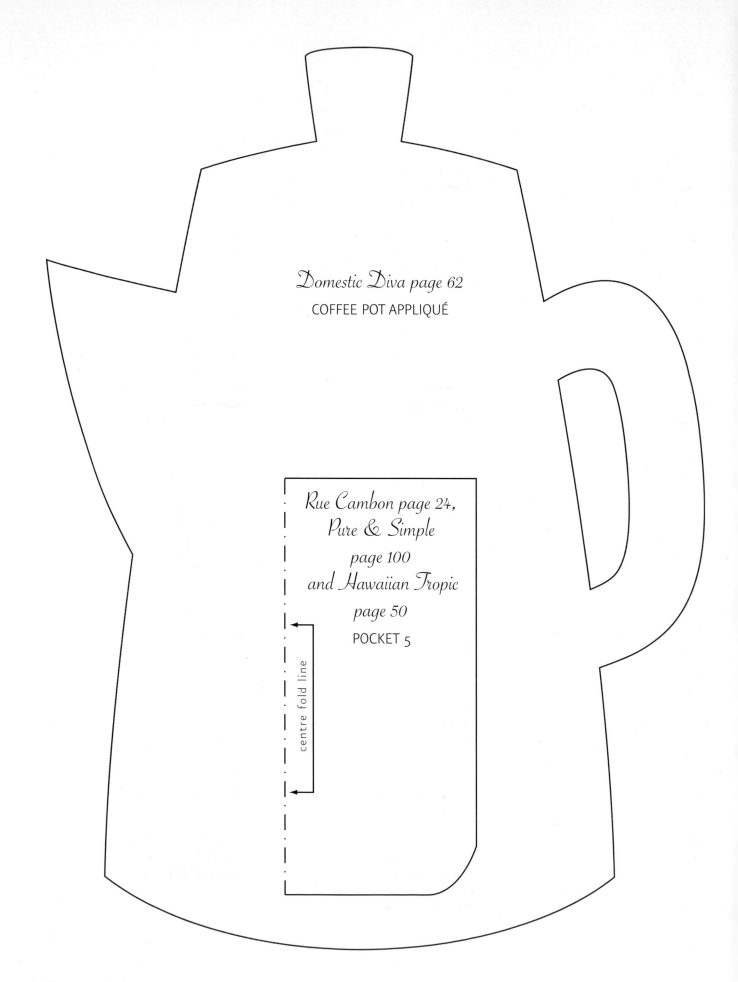

Domestic Diva page 62

COFFEE POT APPLIQUÉ

Rue Cambon page 24,
Pure & Simple

page 100
and Hawaiian Tropic

page 50

POCKET 5

centre fold line

Index

Suppliers

Alexander Furnishings
51-61 Wigmore Street
London W1U 1PU
020 7935 1678

Borovick's
16 Berwick Street
London W1F 0HP
020 7437 2180
www.borovickfabricsltd.co.uk

The Cloth House
47 Berwick Street
London W1F 8SJ
020 7437 5155
www.clothhouse.com

Cloud Cuckoo Land
6 Charlton Place
London N1 8AJ
020 7354 3141

Les Coupons de Saint-Pierre
1 place Saint-Pierre
75018 Paris
00 33 1 42 52 10 79

Dreamtime
6 Pierrepoint Row
Camden Passage
London N1 8EF

La Droguerie
9 & 11 rue du Jour
75001 Paris
00 33 1 45 08 93 27
www.ladroguerie.com

Entrée des Fournisseurs
8 rue des Francs Bourgeois
75003 Paris
00 33 1 48 87 58 98
www.entreedesfournisseurs.com

The French House
41-43 Parsons Green Lane
London SW6 4HH
020 7371 7573
www.thefrenchhouse.co.uk

John Lewis
Oxford Street
London W1A 1EX
020 7629 7711
www.johnlewis.com

Kleins
5 Noel Street
London W1F 8GD
020 7437 6162
www.kleins.co.uk

Liberty
Regent Street
London W1
020 7734 1234
www.liberty.co.uk

MacCulloch & Wallis
25-26 Dering Street
London W15 1AT
020 7629 0311
www.macculloch-wallis.co.uk

Past Caring
54 Essex Road
London N1 8LR

Persiflage
Alfies Antique Market
13-25 Church Street
London NW8 8DT
020 7724 7366

Sew Fantastic
107 Essex Road
London N1 2SL
020 7226 2725

Tissus Reine
3-5 place Saint-Pierre
75018 Paris
00 33 1 46 06 02 31
www.tissus-reine.com

Les Touristes
17 rue des Blancs Manteaux
75004 Paris
00 33 1 42 72 10 84
www.lestouristes.eu

VV Rouleaux
102 Marylebone Lane
London W1U 2QD
020 7224 5179
www.vvrouleaux.com

Acknowledgements

Many, many thanks to Emma Mitchell and Winfried Heinze, great photographers and lots of fun to work with.

Thanks to Trina Dalziel and Stephen Dew for rising to the challenge so magnificently and producing such wonderfully animated illustrations. And to Chris Wood for making the pages look great.

A huge thank you to the team at CICO Books, especially Cindy Richards, for giving me the opportunity to produce this book, to Sally Powell for introducing me to CICO in the first place and her tireless help on the shoots, and to Pete Jorgensen for making sense of it all.

Many thanks to my editor, Marie Clayton, for her essential contribution, and to Annalisa, Betsy, Emily, Felix, Gisela, Kalli, Laura and Lauren for modelling my aprons so well and making them look even more PERFECT.

And, finally, a very special 'thank you' to Luis for just about everything!